ADVENTURE
RACING
GUIDE TO SURVIVAL

Derek Paterson

Acknowledgements

This book wouldn't have been possible without that great, friendly family of adventure racers.

I am indebted to Geoff Hunt and Pascale Lorre, whose event, the Southern Traverse, was the catalyst, and Steve Gurney for his immediate and enthusiastic contribution. Dr Ruth Highet, Shona Jaray and Glenn Muirhead provided professional advice. Many others helped in ways large and small, including: Ian Adamson, Ron Anderson, Mark Burnett, Ox Foster, Bill Godsall, Hadyn Key, John Knight, Neil Jones, Robert Nagle and Viv and Aaron Prince. Murray Vaile at Air New Zealand made sure I got to the Traverses and the organisers of the Raid Gauloises also provided opportunities. Thank you all.

Last but not least, thanks to Spud and Kelly for the fruitcake.

For Rosie
Alex, Bo and Hannah

Published by Sporting Endeavours

This book is copyright. Except for the purpose of fair reviewing, no part of this publication may be reproduced or transmitted in any form or by any means, electronic or mechanical, including photocopying, recording or any information storage and retrieval system, without the prior written permission of the publisher.

ISBN 0-9597769-1-5
Copyright © 1999 Derek Paterson
Design by Stephanie Drew
All photographs by Derek Paterson

Contents

Foreword

It was 10.30 at night, we were tired and we were at the side of the road while a traffic officer wrote us a ticket for speeding through Greymouth. That was bad enough but we were more worried about a dangerous over-loading ticket for the six canoes piled on top of our Citroen. We were lucky, he let us go and we continued on our way to Kumara.

We had answered Robin Judkin's call for competitors in a new event to be called the Coast to Coast. It seemed impossible so to test the waters, literally, we had slipped out of Blenheim and headed south for a look at Goat Pass and the Waimakariri. We had slalom canoes and for the actual race we had resolved to take the mud guards and carriers off our bikes to make them super fast.

During the race itself volunteers were few and far between. The result was that I believe I am the only competitor in the history of the Coast to Coast to have cycled the final leg to Christchurch via Sheffield. Yes, I went straight ahead instead of left after leaving the river at the bridge.

How times have changed. The equipment has improved dramatically with many of the equipment innovations the result of the peculiar demands of today's multisport events. And everyone has them. Now there are a variety of food and drink supplements that greatly improve the performances in endurance events. We also know so much more about the appropriate foods for racing. Not like the first Ironman in Auckland where I gratefully accepted a chocolate chippie biscuit at an aid station on the bike. My clogged and cut mouth couldn't tell the story for the rest of the race !

Perhaps the biggest change is in the minds of the participants. Far more seems achievable. The goals are way beyond what we thought possible in the early 80s. It is like the breaking of the four minute mile. Once it was shown to be possible then many others followed suit and the target was adjusted.

For all of you who are already participants in adventure racing, this book will refresh your preparation and planning as well as bring back many wonderful memories, experiences and friendships. For those of you who already love multisport events — or even just the idea of them — and are ready for the step up to adventure racing, this is the book to inspire and assist you to give it a go and to develop wonderful memories, experiences and friendships.

It has even inspired me to dust off my kayak, to steel myself against the laughter when people see it, and to head back out into our wonderful outdoors.

Have fun and maybe I will see you at Geoff Hunt's next event.

Arthur Klap

Arthur Klap is the only athlete to have competed in the first Coast to Coast and the first New Zealand Ironman. Since then he has organised over 200 triathlons, including the World Triathlon Championships, and continues to compete and train others.

Introduction

Hurricane force winds hurl snow in their faces, like ice blasted from a catapult. It's two hours after midnight but even in daylight vision would be impossible.

Standing upright invites being blown over and stopping is suicidal. There's no alternative but to carry on, clawing a way through the maelstrom, with occasional glances at a compass to try and check direction, hoping, praying the pass is near, they're on the right route — and that once over, they'll be out of the shrieking winds. Perhaps they'll find shelter and finally be able to rest until daylight. Maybe even sleep. There have only been a few snatched hours in the last three days and those came sheltering from a similarly frigid, cyclonic, night-time blast on exposed ridges. When trying to ride mountain bikes.

Welcome to adventure racing — or expedition racing as it is also sometimes called — a multi-day, multi-discipline team's race through harsh, inhospitable and beautiful lands. From sea level to icy mountain wastes, rain forests to desiccated desert, teams "move when they can and sleep when they dare." And come back year after year. Most come not to win but to challenge themselves, their bodies, their minds and their spirits. And to meet again like-minded individuals more interested in open spaces, people and physical and mental challenges than in the latest toys hyped by commercial propaganda.

Which is not to say this is some kind of hair-shirt, back-to-basics brigade. Far from it. These guys — and girls — use the latest technology –food and drink, shoes, clothes, packs, sleeping bags and so on — where appropriate. But the most successful competitors are self-reliant, able to adapt quickly to changing conditions and circumstances. They do not have to rely on the technology. As Hadyn Key says, "In the pack of every Kiwi, you'll find a coat hangar and a piece of No8 wire."

So it comes as no surprise who the best adventure racers are. When the Kiwis compete, there is usually a separate race for the minor placings. Kiwis grow up learning self-reliance and the skills necessary for the sport. They learn to move in the hills and how to find their way in inclement weather through harsh, unforgiving terrain. They paddle kayaks, climb rocks and mountains and ride bicycles everywhere. And they learn to be adaptable, to find solutions with minimal materials. It is, if you like, 'the No8 wire solution.'

These skills are honed to perfection in weekend races and events like the Southern Traverse here in New Zealand. And shown internationally in the Raid Gauloises, the original adventure race, and the EcoChallenge — when the Kiwis can afford to go.

Adventure races — and their shorter, older sibling, multisport — are gaining in popularity in many places. In France, the United States, Great Britain, Canada, Germany, Japan, Australia, South Africa and even Argentina and Brazil it is possible to find an event every month, if not every weekend. In the US in particular, there are series of shorter races, lasting just a few hours, running nation-wide and one sponsor is pushing for Olympic recognition. As popularity grows, so does commercial interest. The EcoChallenge, for example, one of the two big international adventure races, is sponsored by Discovery Channel. The Raid Gauloises also gets hours of television coverage at home in France and throughout Europe and the US.

It is harder here in New Zealand, of course, where the sports sponsorship dollars seem to go mostly to rugby, both union and league, cricket and yachting. Despite this, the sport is growing fast, especially with disillusioned triathletes discovering the camaraderie of multisport which leads in turn to the longer adventure races. And Kiwis are even more dominant internationally in these events than in the more traditional sports. Steve Gurney and John Howard are household names in millions of homes across the US and Europe.

Adventure racing is the fastest growing team sport in the world. On one side, as one racer puts it, "the sport is becoming a real time TV adventure driven by the media. And the athletes are the poor, underpaid actors."

But the sport has huge appeal, much more than any one of the several disciplines encompassed or even triathlon, whose popularity appears to have peaked or even passed. It appeals to people of all ages from many, diverse backgrounds. Ian Adamson, one of adventure racing's titans, puts it this way: "It offers people who never excelled at the anaerobic, redline sports an opportunity to compete using skill, teamwork and intelligence against their more athletically gifted counterparts. Adventure racing is a sport for intelligent people and those seeking a more holistic experience than simply dashing around a marked race course."

This book will help you make that next step, the transition into adventure racing.

Teams against the clock

Multisport had its beginnings here in New Zealand in 1980, around the same time as triathlon, when Robin Judkins organised the first Alpine Ironman events, initially in Wanaka and then moving north to Mt Hutt. Others picked up the idea and races began appearing all the way up country to Mt Ruapehu. These races typically involved some or all of skiing, running, kayaking and cycling. Sometimes an uphill component was included, from the base lodge to the summit ridge at Mt Hutt, for example, or the top of the Knoll Ridge to the Crater Lake on Ruapehu.

New events kept appearing, especially in the South Island. Swimming events quickly became triathlons with their own followings, finding particular favour in the North Island and the cities. Multisport was a triathlon for non-swimmers, according to one cynical view. The two groups split and went their separate ways, each with its own association. Triathlon became fiercely competitive and entered the Olympic arena. Ironman, with its much longer distances, has its own aficionados and has settled into a series round the world (the New Zealand link has just, very successfully, shifted to Taupo) with a final at its birthplace in Hawaii. In both these events New Zealand athletes have been very competitive, too, with the likes of the legendary Erin Baker, Rick Wells, Jenny Rose, Sarah Harrow, John Hellemans, Scott Balance, John Knight in the Ironman and, currently, Hamish Carter.

Multisport, on the other hand, maintained its more earthy image of co-operation rather than competition, sport for the pleasure of it, not to win at all costs, sharing ideas, plans and even equipment mid-race. The Coast to Coast, brainchild of the irrepressible, manic Judkins, was born in 1983 and introduced a new concept, that of spreading a race over two days. Almost single-handedly, Judkins had created the climate that allowed multisport — and ultimately adventure racing — to grow. All multisporters owe him a debt of gratitude for making their sport a commercially viable proposition and thus ensuring its continued existence.

The next, and crucial, advance came in 1989, courtesy of French adventurer and journalist Gerard Fusil, who had had a 'vision' while on assignment in Patagonia. Judkins allowed two person teams in the Coast to Coast, each completing two of the four legs — cycling and kayaking or mountain running and cycling. Fusil introduced three new concepts — teams of five, including at least one woman (being French and thus, some would say, a chauvinist by definition, his prescription allowed an all women team but not all men), all of whom must keep together and finish together, in a race lasting several days and covering hundreds of kilometres passing through a number of Check Points that must first be located, a navigation problem. The Raid Gauloises was born. And so, too, was adventure racing.

Appropriately enough, the first Raid took place here in New Zealand in 1989 on a course suggested by Dave Bamford, of Wellington. Beginning at Lake Ohau, the contestants, mostly French or French domiciled and Kiwi, traversed some of the most rugged and beautiful landscapes in the country to reach Lake Manapouri for the final paddle to the finish.

First across the line? Kiwis, of course, including John Howard and Steve Gurney, both now international adventure racing legends. After an epic cat and mouse battle over treacherous terrain and through testing weather, Kiwi teams took the first four places. Steve went on to become New Zealand's first professional multisporter, eking out a precarious existence at home and mostly unable to raise the sponsorship to contest the more lucrative international races. John, quieter, at least until you know him, and more introspective, had precisely the right kind of mental approach and attitude. Mark Burnett, founder of the EcoChallenge, has been quoted as calling him the "Michael Jordan of adventure racing."

But what, exactly, is an adventure race? It is an event that challenges individuals physically and mentally yet it is teams which are important, teams which must remain together at all times. Each team carries a 'passport' that must be stamped as each Check Point is passed in a set order. Every so often they will reach an Assistance Point or Transition Area where team assistants will have prepared food and readied clothing and equipment for a new mode of travel, for the next stage. The EcoChallenge, however, has done away with assistants. Instead, teams must prepare everything themselves, before the race starts. All their gear is transferred from transition to transition by the organisers. There is no motorised transport for competitors (although planes have been used in the Raid to allow skydiving) and power is usually human — on foot, bike, kayak, raft — and occasionally horse, camel or sail.

Burnett describes adventure racing as "a non-stop, non-motorised, team based expedition with a stopwatch."

The races themselves take place far from the comforts and accoutrements of civilisation. Teams are on their own, they must carry sufficient food to survive, sometimes for days at a time, often in atrocious weather, moving constantly and navigating through harsh terrain that can punish mistakes severely, even fatally. Fortunately, this has not happened yet although Steve Gurney spent more than a week in a coma on life support after winning the Sarawak Raid. Travelling through the vast Mulu cave system, he contracted leptospirosis from the guano of the millions of bats that live in the caves and defecate into the underground streams, the infection entering his body through the many inevitable scratches and cuts. His was the worst case of several that year. Recovery was slow but he is once again one of the world's elite adventure racers.

Routes have traversed mountains and deserts, jungles and lakes, caves, rivers and the sea itself.

The Raid and the EcoChallenge, the two biggest events, have had their success more or less guaranteed with massive sponsorships and worldwide television audiences. Both use exotic locations. The Raid went from New Zealand to Costa Rica, New Caledonia, Oman, Madagascar, Sarawak, Patagonia, South Africa, Ecuador and the tenth, in the year 2000, will start in Tibet, traverse Nepal and finish on the plains of India. The EcoChallenge has gone from Utah to British Columbia, Cairns, Morocco and, later in 1999, will go to Patagonia.

The Southern Traverse is the third leg of an international adventure racing triumvirate but it is the poor cousin in comparison. Race organiser Geoff Hunt is a relentless international competitor, tenacious and full of enthusiasm and drive but he lacks the charisma of, for example, Robin Judkins.

But the Southern Traverse has two major advantages. That first Raid showed the suitability of the terrain but it had barely scratched the surface. The Southern Alps of New Zealand cover a greater land area than the more famous Alps of Europe in France, Switzerland, Germany, Austria and Italy. There are new opportunities over every ridge and down (or up) every valley. And second, there is the astounding commitment and capability of the Kiwi contestants. These abilities grow out of the basic familiarity with the hills, the annual 10 day hikes through the Southern Alps, often in appalling conditions. Superlative map reading, mountain walking, river crossing and sometimes rope skills are sometimes essential and constantly honed. This builds stamina and the ability to keep moving in treacherous terrain, often carrying heavy loads, and to make quick and accurate decisions at times of extreme fatigue. Couple this with a basic 'do-it-yourself, fix-it-with-whatever-you've-got' philosophy ('the No8-wire solution') and faith in your companions, sometimes entrusting them with your life, and you have perfect initial training for the multi-day, multi-discipline adventure races.

Even so, the first years were hard and Hunt had to work elsewhere to support his dream of the Southern Traverse.

Meanwhile, the Raid was growing in size and importance. The Americans had followed the Belgians into regular entry. In 1994, in Sarawak, curiously on another course designed with Dave Bamford's assistance, there were the usual French, Belgian and American teams lined up at the start. Alongside them were teams from Japan, Germany, Singapore and Australia and a couple of 'local' outfits. To shore up these inexperienced locals, who'd never done anything like this before, three 'hired guns' were imported from New Zealand. John Howard and Steve Gurney joined three Sarawakians and Viv Prince ended up with a more eclectic bunch that included an Irish pilot working in Sarawak and a Hong Kong banker.

Some people rely on their equipment, arriving with cutting edge, ultra-lightweight packs and shoes. Howard and Gurney arrived with the packs they'd used when winning that first Raid five years earlier. They took their three companions, passed on some rudimentary skills in the day or so available before the start and then proceeded to teach them on the fly how to read and interpret maps, think on their feet and keep moving. They also themselves received a lesson during the race on cave navigation. The result was that the organisers barely had time to set up Check Points before the Kiwi/Malaysia team came storming through.

The adventure racing world took note and when no Kiwis turned up in Patagonia the constant question was: "Didn't they come because of the nuclear bomb tests in Mururoa?" The answer was a more prosaic lack of funds and sponsorship. In the meantime, they more or less made the EcoChallenge their own, either in Kiwi teams or providing those essentially Kiwi skills of improvisation and adaptability as individuals in other teams.

Questions were asked. "What makes them so good?" "Is it the milk?" "Is it the sheep?" "Is it the water?" The best way to find out, of course, was to come and see and perhaps, by osmosis, key ingredients and essential skills could be learned on the Kiwis' proving ground. The internationals started coming and the Southern Traverse began to be held in the same regard as the longer Raid and EcoChallenge.

International interest, unfortunately, did not turn into instant success, at least not in commercial terms. Teams and individuals from England, France, the US, Australia, Japan and even Brazil began to appear and ever more Kiwis were attracted, showing the depth of talent

More than anything else, the Southern Traverse has gained a reputation as a competitors' course, a very technical course, according to one experienced American racer, perhaps because Hunt is one of the top international adventure racers himself, with top five finishes in both the Raid and EcoChallenge. As an active racer he knows intimately what appeals and, even more importantly, what will challenge and ultimately give lasting satisfaction and a sense of achievement. For that is another, unique side to the Traverse. Each course is designed so that legs can be shortened or dropped altogether to allow slower teams the pleasure of crossing the finish line.

Adventure racing is not an 'anaerobic redline sport.' It is about skill, mental and physical, team work and intelligence. It is no wonder it is the fastest growing team sport in the world today.

Note: Afraid that the term 'adventure racing' has been hijacked to cover events that don't meet his criteria, EcoChallenge founder Mark Burnett has begun calling his event an 'expedition race.'

Mental and physical strength

Anybody, well, almost anybody, with a sense of adventure and a sense of humour can be an adventure racer. Very few of you — of us — will ever be in the top echelon but isn't that true of all sports, of all endeavours? Yet we all run or bike or climb or play tennis or chess without ever expecting to be world champion.

We do these things for fun, because we enjoy doing them. Pleasure and enjoyment should be very high on the list of realistic goals for any adventure racer.

All racers, however, share one trait in particular, a love, a passion for the outdoors. It is, as Steve Gurney puts it, a question of lifestyle. Practically all the most successful adventure racers hold down full time jobs — maybe they have to, it can be very expensive without a deep-pocketed sponsor, certainly at the top level — but they've grown up with the outdoors. Holidays were spent at the beach or lake and they made long hikes through the mountains, skiing and ski touring there in the winter. And they go there still, whenever they can.

Some people even organise their business schedules to suit. Ron Anderson, a committed adventure racer and successful businessman, organises board meetings in the mountains, at lakes and so on so that any free time can be used for a climb, a paddle or a run. There is a company culture supporting the sport and these occasions keep them all fit and help to bond them both as sports teams and business units, a double benefit.

You can see the outdoors background in the top Kiwi adventure racers. Geoff Hunt, Southern Traverse founder and race director, gave up university for the mountains. For many years he skied and rafted for a living, perfect training for adventure sport. John Howard climbed mountains in many places, including Cotopaxi in Ecuador which, to his bitter disappointment, he was unable to summit again in the Ecuador Raid Gauloises. He also lined up for the very first Alpine Ironman events. He has been part of the sport from its infancy and remains the world's most successful adventure racer. Hadyn Key discovered skiing and then Queenstown, New Zealand's (some would say the world's) adventure capital, where he still lives, pursuing the outdoor lifestyle with a vengeance. Ron Anderson was a hunter, clambering through the rugged mountains of Fiordland. Now he retreats there to his own mountain hut whenever he can.

For people like this, adventure racing is simply an extension of their normal lifestyle — or how they would ideally like their life to be. It provides a challenge, and the best racers love new challenges and achieving the solutions necessary to overcome the problem.

More and more racers are coming into the sport from triathlon and occasionally from single sport backgrounds like cycling or running, especially harriers and mountain running. Their reasons are varied but for some it is the welcome change from endlessly ploughing up and down a swimming pool, running the same old roads and tracks, cycling the same places.

Adventure racing gives back the challenge. In fact, it creates a number of new challenges. Training, too, has to become more varied. You have to run up and down hills, through bush and over rocks, riding is best on mountain bikes on gnarly single track or long excursions into the hills and you get to paddle down ever changing rivers or in the surf.

John Knight is a classic example. For nearly six years he travelled the world competing in up to six Iron Man events a year. He was world class with best results a first in France and a third in Lanzarote. He was training for 40 to 50 hours a week and then, less than two weeks before the Iron Man in New Zealand in 1994, he had a bike crash and began the race with his hand still in bandages. Halfway through the bike section he pulled out. The fun had gone.

Back in 1990 he'd competed in the Xerox Challenge, a multisport race nearly a month long from the top of New Zealand to the bottom. "It was an adventure, it was different, it was something that had never been done before." But the Iron Man still came first and it wasn't until 1994 he finally competed in the Southern Traverse — and hasn't missed since. "I do it for enjoyment, for the pleasure of it. I've never done the Coast to Coast, it doesn't seem enjoyable to me, too intense, too much like the Iron Man." Not enough fun.

Other newcomers are sick of the hype and pettiness, the win at all costs mentality. They are amazed and delighted to discover the welcoming family of adventure racers. It is one of the greatest attributes of this sport, the remarkable camaraderie that suffuses any gathering, the willingness to pitch in and help, offering advice or gear as necessary.

What, then, are the qualities necessary to be a successful adventure racer? As Ian Adamson, one of the world's very top athletes, says, "You have to be a good generalist." In other words, ability in just one skill isn't enough. You may be a fantastic mountain biker but if you can't paddle a kayak, you'll get left far behind and possibly fatigued and hypothermic from frequent immersion in ice cold mountain water.

The top adventure racers also belong to single sports clubs, too, bike clubs being particular beneficiaries. Being a member of your local mountain bike group will get you riding on regular outings and let you pick up training, tips and skills from the club experts. You'll also learn a lot more about equipment. There are always technical 'experts' who have to have the latest, if not the greatest, piece of gear. You'll see if it works. Or not. And you'll learn practical maintenance skills. The local kayak group likewise gives you the opportunity to learn new skills and improve technique. Then there are the regular trips and competitions to hone those new-found skills. You could also try harriers or, even better, find a mountain running club. Tramping and hiking clubs, of course, provide a steady diet of trips into the hills and there are always people waiting to push the limits a little bit harder, go faster, lighter and further. Just the practice you need. And don't forget the orienteering.

Wherever there's competition, you need to be part of it. It remains the best way of testing and proving skills. While it is not necessary to excel in every sport, although admittedly many of the best adventure racers do excel in individual sports, you do need good, consistent results. The better you can be in each discipline, the better your chances will be in adventure racing.

Remember, too, that while being good at a particular skill may not actually win you the race, being bad or unskilled will ensure you don't even finish or set you so far back you have to finish on a shortened course.

Skills and techniques can be practised and honed in multisport competition, smaller events of a few hours duration. Every time you compete you can learn something or have an idea reinforced. It might be about route finding, nutrition, mountain bike downhilling, paddling, reading the river or transitions. Learn it, apply it and practise it.

You need to be very aware of what's happening in transitions, have systems in place that work, that see you fed, changed and back on the course in the shortest time or under a blanket catching up on sleep. There are probably more adventure races won or lost in transitions than anywhere else. Split times will often show teams have broadly similar stage results but vastly different times in transitions.

So, it is the solid, consistent results in each discipline coupled with practised transitions that give the results and ultimately the satisfaction. The satisfaction of just finishing, if that is your goal, is as real as that of winning. And you have to be realistic.

At present, and with only a few exceptions, the top adventure racers are all in their mid-30s to mid-40s, like Steve Gurney and John Howard, who won that seminal adventure race the Grand Traverse in 1989 and are still virtually unbeatable. Many others, in New Zealand, France, the US and elsewhere, started around the same time. What all these people brought with them, besides their backgrounds in kayaking, mountaineering, running, multisport or whatever, was a certain level of maturity.

Physical maturity brings endurance but it is mental maturity that is truly critical to success in adventure racing and it is this which separates the top teams from the rest.

What is mental maturity? For a start, there is the realisation that personal success will only come with team effort, there is no place for prima donnas. This is what makes team dynamics and team culture such an interesting field of study. There are all too many instances of team members being abandoned, sometimes in dire circumstances. Other teams, perhaps with individually less talented athletes, have succeeded beyond their own — and anyone else's — expectations because of their commitment, compassion, respect for each other and ability to communicate.

Ox Foster takes this even further by saying there are many ways to maintain wellbeing but communication with your team mates is the critical one. Loads can be shared, sore feet attended to and so on long before they become a problem to the detriment of the team.

Assistance within the team has to come with good cause, of course. Individuals still have to be tough, resourceful, positive and not given easily to complaining. It may well be a team mate who first notices a potential problem, a slight change in your gait or paddling style, loss of balance or being a bit slower up the hills.

You must be able to relax, too, no matter how difficult the situation or what the level of stress. Again, the power of positive thinking, the ability to see beyond the moment, is required. You have to be able to say, "I'm hurting now but we're near the transition and then I can sit down and paddle." A state of sleep deprivation and fatigue quickly becomes normal in adventure racing and you must be able to adjust to this. To quote Ian Adamson again: "You must have the ability to make good, fast decisions under the pressure of competition, fatigue, sleep deprivation and emotional distress." And adjust that decision if conditions change. Sometimes the whole team makes these choices jointly. Other times it is the team captain who binds the team, sees that all members contribute to the best of their ability and maintains a sense of happiness and wellbeing.

Navigation, a mental discipline, is most critical to adventure racing success. Honing cycling or paddling skills may see your team a few minutes faster through a section. On the other hand, a navigation error can cost several hours in time and a lot of energy. Quick and accurate route choice can be difficult under pressure. It is far harder when tired and sleep deprived, two hours before dawn in the pouring rain on the side of a mountain. The wrong choice may be fatal. The best solution may even be to stop and sleep. Another choice.

It is, arguably, sufficient to have just one quality navigator on the team but what happens if they're tired or injured? The more people to share the load, the easier it will be for everybody. The top teams usually share navigation duties and make joint decisions at times of doubt or crisis. They can find their way in open country and in dense forest, at night and during the day, in good weather and when the conditions are atrocious. Remember, too, the best navigators don't just know how to reach a co-ordinate on a map, they're also always aware of where precisely they are on that map at all times.

Good map reading skills provide another advantage. They may well allow you to determine where you can find water and thus save you precious weight by reducing the amount of fluid you need to carry.

In short, you need to be a good all-rounder and a team player, able to work within as well as augment the unit. You need the mental strength to be able to continue in the face of adversity, to know where you are and to know when to stop and when to start again. Survival skills are crucial. You need to be fit and with great endurance, with the stamina, again mental and physical, to push yourself over these extra days. Your body seems to have its own memory of earlier days of pushing hard and that helps to keep you going.

There's something to learn in every race. You can never know it all.

Fitness, skills and training

By Steve Gurney

Non-athletic friends and acquaintances often suggest that adventure racing must be the ultimate sport masochism and they wonder how and why I do it. But I can see in their eyes the secret envy they have for my adventures when I talk about them.

The truth is, they unnecessarily put adventure racing in the too hard basket for it is actually achievable by anyone with a sense of adventure and a little fitness (and maybe a sense of humour).

There are two extremes. At the top level are the athletes with a very high level of base fitness. For them, it is often a kind of lifestyle as they are the people who go away into the hills whenever they can, whether hiking, climbing, paddling, mountain biking, hunting or ski touring. At the other extreme are the hobby racers, in it just for the adventure, the pleasure and satisfaction of competing and being out in the wild. They're in it just to finish, not to win.

Whichever category you're aiming for, when you have finished working through this chapter, you will have a better understanding of the principals of training to prepare yourself for the Southern Traverse and other multi-sport and adventure races. You'll know some of the techniques and have knowledge of some of the skills you'll need to practise to compete safely and enjoyably.

An adventure race is not like a triathlon on a pre-determined course with predictable conditions. It is almost the complete opposite, unpredictable in length and conditions, in short, an adventure.

Fitness

What is adventure racing fitness? It is not being able to run 100m in 10secs. It is not doing an aerobics class at the gym. And it is not even running a marathon in 2hrs 10 mins. Adventure racing fitness is more of a rugged fitness, it is about having the endurance to keep racing for 24 hours or even up to nine or ten days. It is about being able to move swiftly and without stopping on rough terrain. This is very important.

For example, running on smooth surfaces uses predominantly the major muscle groups. But if you're running on uneven ground, there is the process of proprioception where information is fed to the brain and then messages are sent back to the stabiliser or auxiliary muscles to stabilise the ankles when there is an uneven foot strike. This same reflex action is applicable in other activities such as mountain biking and kayaking in rough conditions when minute corrections are, with practise, automatically made. You don't get this running on level ground, cycling on smooth tarmac or paddling on flat water. The message is, then, that you have to train these stabilising muscles in your preparations for adventure racing.

Adventure racing fitness is also about operating efficiently in extremes of weather. Blood viscosity and muscle elasticity and function change between cold and hot weather. When the temperature drops, the veins and capillaries narrow, vaso-constriction, so the outer tissue gets less blood, oxygen and other goodies that are carried in it, leading to less efficient performance. And in cold weather, just like a rubber band, muscles don't stretch as easily and are more prone to injury. Blood and other cellular liquids cool and become slightly thicker. At the opposite extreme, in warm weather, we tend to operate more efficiently but as conditions get hotter and hotter, we need to combat the heat with improved fluid intake to avoid dehydration. You have to train to cope with both of these extremes because they can occur in the same race, even a few hours apart. You have to learn to eat and drink on the go and to wear the right clothing. You have to practise all this in training, leaving nothing to chance on race day.

But more than anything, adventure racing fitness is about mental fitness, the ability to cope with seemingly endless roads ahead, the ability to cope with the knowledge your body is going to be required to keep performing for hours and hours and hours without rest. There is also the need for your brain to keep working efficiently through the night with little sleep, through those times of night which are traditionally sleep times, especially between 2 and 4 o'clock in the morning when your body is at its lowest ebb.

It is also about operating out of your comfort zone. For example, you need to be able to cope with the frustration of continuing over a mountain pass with all your clothing under the parka and overtrou wet and uncomfortable and with no chance to change them until the next transition which may be hours or even days away. Again, you have to practise this, learn to be comfortable with discomfort.

Specificity

I consider this to be the most important part of physical (as opposed to mental) adventure race training and I always remember the Boy Scout motto: "Be prepared." You have to be prepared for anything and everything the course and the weather may throw at you. These events are typically held in the mountains where the weather is always changeable. An easy course can very quickly become a difficult course with a sudden change in the weather.

You can bet your last Leppin the course will be less than ideal, somewhere along the way. It may be a change in the weather, an overcast night blocking the moon or even the batteries in your headlamp failing. My point here is that it is important to train in all weather conditions, that you're not a 'fair weather trainer' who looks out the window, sees the rain and decides to wait until the sun has come out. Train in sun, wind and rain, go out and train whenever you've scheduled it, not when there's a break in the bad weather. If you have to reschedule, make the occasional training session in the worst possible weather you're likely to encounter in the race. You'll be glad of this preparation come race time.

But in recommending this, I'm suddenly getting nervous. You have to look after your own safety. We're talking about pushing the envelope but not exceeding it. It's important to check the weather forecast to see how bad things are going to get. In other words, its better to be going out in a reducing storm rather than one that's building up. You should take with you a repair kit and emergency clothes and food.

Always ask yourself: "What if ...?" If, for example, you fell out of your kayak, are you going to be blown out to sea? Or on to shore? In other words, plan carefully and safely in case everything doesn't go according to plan. Tell someone where you're going, leave a message and arrange to call someone when you're back so they'll know where to go looking if you don't return. If you're going to push the envelope, make sure you've got a backstop. I don't want to read about you in the paper.

Now is a good time to bring in mental pre-play. Think about all possible scenarios that could occur during a race and go and practise them. If it's hot weather, ask yourself, "What bits of equipment and special training do I need to perform better in this kind of weather?" Or if you want to practise night navigating, try doing it also in the wind and rain or even whiteout so it's a real indication of what it might be like in the race.

Remember that adventure racing isn't just about physical fitness. Mental fitness is perhaps even more important. Much like an orienteering course, adventure races are designed to reward those who pause to calculate an efficient or even clever way to do things. Training should include this mentality. In training, set yourself little orienteering or adventure courses so you can practise choosing options and even see which is fastest.

An interesting and fun training method I do is to go out with another person, each of us with a handful of coloured ribbons. We each have an orienteering map and we arrange a meeting place about 10-15 minutes away. Going separate ways, we mark on the map where we've tied our ribbons. At the meeting place, we swap maps and run back, collecting the other person's ribbons. We might do three or four of these exercises in one session. It's a lot of fun. You learn a lot about navigation, about map reading and route choice, and you get the bonus of a good run.

Be innovative in your training, try it in other disciplines and you might come up with some other games, too. It all makes training more fun and you're more likely to keep doing it.

I also strongly recommend training with packs, just like you'd carry in the race. Even if it's just a 40 minute run or ride, it is beneficial to take a pack with you and also to wear the kind of gear you'll be wearing in the race, right down to the hydration systems and drink bottles you plan on using. I often load my pack with telephone books, bricks or bottles of water. But if you're going out for a longer training session, perhaps lasting several hours, it might be even better to take along things that might be useful to you out there, like rain jackets, water, sunscreen and a lot of food.

Do this for all disciplines, in all weathers and while you do it, mentally visualise yourself doing it in actual race conditions, thinking carefully about the things you've got with you and what you might want to have.

In summary, don't be one of our fair weather friends. Get tough.

Injury prevention and safety

The golden rule is, of course, "Prevention is far better than cure."

The most important thing regarding injury prevention is to launch or build slowly into your training schedule, especially with new activities. I must emphasise that when you start something new, you should begin with short sessions otherwise you'll get injured or at the least be very sore for days. This means you have to control your enthusiasm. In the excitement of adventure racing training it is very easy to get carried away with it all. I recommend adhering to the training schedules, which appear in the next chapter, where we talk about periodisation. Stick very carefully to your periodisation so there is a structured and gradual build up.

When you launch into something new, I suggest 15 minutes the first time and build up incrementally by five or ten minutes in subsequent sessions. It is very, very important to allow recovery here, too. You'll do a hard or a long session after which you feel quite sore. It's very important you don't go out and do another hard session until you're totally recovered from the first one. It might even mean leaving it for as long as a week. It's typically only two or three days for recovery but to prevent injury, you must really listen to your body.

I strongly recommend getting expert advice if you're starting out on a new discipline. Instruction is a very good investment, especially for the first couple of sessions so you don't pick up and train with bad habits. And, when you begin training with weight in your pack, this should also be an incremental increase, starting with an empty pack, perhaps with a jacket, and building up slowly to full race weight of 8-10 kg.

Equally important is a warm-up before your sessions. You must give your body a warning it's going to go through a work out and I recommend 15 minutes minimum of warm-up, of slow and easy of the discipline you are doing. A good indication of being ready is when you start to sweat. If you have an injury or some tight spots, warm up for longer or until the tight spot has eased. If you're still tied up after 15-20 minutes, it's better you put off that particular session.

As part of your warm-up you could include stretching. You should include stretching somewhere in your session but definitely not when you're cold. Stretch only when you've warmed up or at the end of your session. Cold muscles don't stretch very well. In fact, as already mentioned, they're likely to break, just like a rubber band stretched beyond its limits.

Training and exercise, especially the intense exercise that you'll be doing in the hills, shortens muscles and they become less flexible so that when called upon to execute an extreme movement, the muscles may not respond and injury may result. The aim of any stretching routine is to lengthen muscles, tendons and other tissues so that movement does not cause excessive strain.

Stretching is not bouncing. It should be a sustained, pain-free stretch for a minimum of 10 seconds.

Adventure racing, by definition, is riskier than a 'straight' triathlon and that's what makes it interesting, what adds to the challenge. Without risk it could be boring. However, it is important to calculate the risk to ensure your own safety.

Remember, you want to push the boundaries but you don't want to cross them which could lead to injury or, possibly, something even worse.

Be a thinking athlete. Every time you enter a dangerous situation calculate whether it is safe to continue. To move the odds in your favour, you'll need to improve your skills through training and, to complete the circle, you need specific training that will improve those skills.

Also to improve the odds, you can take an 'Oh shit kit' with you. It doesn't have to be big but it might include an emergency blanket, an extra muesli bar or Leppin, polypropylene gloves and hat, they're only tiny, and a metre or so of duct tape. If you're on a bike you'll need a puncture repair kit, a chain breaker and Allen keys. In the kayak you might want something to dry off the hull before you repair it. And as already said, tell someone where you're going and leave an intentions note so they'll know where to find you if you don't make it back.

And it is worth repeating: check the weather forecast.

Now it's time to consider what happens if you do get injured in training. This can often be devastating and depressing for someone with a well-structured training schedule when they're building up to the big race of the season. I've found the best way to combat this is to immediately seek expert advice. That is, make an appointment as soon as possible to see your doctor or physiotherapist to plan a course for full recovery. They're well qualified to give you a constructive path back to recovery or advise you if the injury is too serious and you have to pull out of the race. Whatever the outcome, you'll have taken a positive step towards remedying the injury and you'll feel better for it.

Don't just sit there thinking it might go away.

Skills

Navigation

Navigation is common to all disciplines in the Southern Traverse and adventure racing in general. In fact, when it comes to racing, it is the single most important skill — and the most exciting, too. Here is a list that will improve your navigation skills:

▼ Join an orienteering club.

▼ Instead of just running, take a map of a forest park or other public land, mark three or four points on the map, identify them and connect them on your run.

▼ Do as many rogaines as you can (rogaining is similar to orienteering, pass as many check points as you can in a given period, often 3, 6, 12 or 24 hours. Night rogaining is especially beneficial as it takes you through the time you are at your lowest ebb, and thus more closely approximates adventure racing) as you can. In fact, do as many events as you can.

▼ Rather than tramp or hike on a track, travel cross-country to a valley or a peak identified on a map.

▼ Practise night time navigation as this is a very different skill. You may not be able to see peaks and hills to orient yourself so you have to know exactly where you are on the map (24 hour rogaining obviously helps here).

▼ Go out at night in the rain, fog and wind. It will happen in the race and psychologically you'll be prepared, happier in the knowledge you can do it.

▼ Take the opportunity to read maps at all times, even when travelling in a car so you know exactly where you are on the road map. It is all good navigation practice.

▼ At home, select a point on a map and visualise the terrain around it as you rotate through 360 degrees. This is visual imagery, learning to interpret what is on the map. You may be able to confirm this later on a run or a hike.

▼ Two of you set separate courses with ribbons, as described previously.

▼ Play with a GPS if you have access to one. This will confirm a position you've plotted on the map. I repeat, it is extremely important to know exactly where you are at all times.

▼ On a ski field or snow area you're familiar with (and where it's safe), try navigating in a whiteout.

▼ Try navigating in dense bush (but be as environmentally friendly as possible).

▼ Getting maps can be a problem but that's where the orienteering clubs come in, they often have a selection of maps (but remember to get permission if you're on private land). Remember, though, the maps in the race may be a different scale and you have to get used to that, too. Race maps will inevitably be a larger scale than orienteering maps.

Running

This is almost a misnomer as there is very little fast running, perhaps just when you're trying to make a deadline, like getting to a point before a dark zone begins, or to pass another team. For top teams, for 70 percent of the time it's usually just a brisk walking pace, 25 percent a gentle jog on the flat or downhill and 5 percent running to make deadlines.

▼ I still advocate running in training, however, especially during the week. Weekends, with their longer sessions of several hours to overnight, can be a combination of walking and running. Maintain that brisk pace, simulate race conditions and don't take long breaks. You can do some exciting trips. Tramps that might take the average hiker three or four days you can do in one or two. Remember, take a pack full of race-type gear, even for the short runs.

▼ Training in the hills is very important as this is where adventure races usually take place. Hills typically are very long and you need to reflect this in your training.

▼ Practise orienteering. Even if you are just running, take a map with you and identify where you are all the time. You could even check bearings with a compass.

▼ Running should be on tracks and rocks. As explained above, this exercises and trains the stabiliser muscles. The idea is to train for the worst conditions possible so anything easier is going to be a piece of cake. Avoid the roads as you'll seldom be on them in the race and, in any case, they'll be easy after trail running training. It's also good for injury prevention to keep off the road.

▼ You also need to practise night running. It can be fun and exciting and tracks you've become bored with running on suddenly become new terrain and you'll probably even find it difficult to recognise them. You'll need to invest in a good headlamp, such as a halogen lamp. The amount of light determines your speed and I would recommend a high powered bike lamp if you want to run really fast. It goes without saying you need to go out in bad weather, on rough ground and in dense bush.

▼ You may wonder about me and think I've come from a circus but I find balance exercises very useful for strengthening the ankles and increasing your speed over tricky terrain like rocks (it will also improve balance on your mountain bike). Run as fast as you can along the curb, the top of a wall, railings — anything you can find. The trick is to look ahead as far as you can. The further you look, the faster you can run. I also have some wires set up in the backyard for tightrope practice. You can use fences, chains between posts and so on.

Water skills

The Southern Traverse is often on New Zealand's coldest and roughest lakes and sometimes the ocean. In other words, you have to be prepared for big waves. On rivers, you have to learn to identify hazards such as trees, rapids, boils and eddies.

You also need to be proficient in different water craft. In the Southern Traverse you use mainly kayaks, singles and doubles. Rafts have been used. Overseas races can also include canoes, usually inflatables, but a reasonable simulation in training is Canadian canoes as inflatables are hard to find in New Zealand.

▼ For beginners, there's a lot to learn to become proficient at water skills. Joining a kayak club is a great start for the wealth of experience and skills among members. They have regular weekend trips where you can learn a lot quite quickly. Coaching and technique training are also available.

▼ You need to learn an efficient forward technique as well as support strokes, draw strokes and perhaps even rolling, which can save time in the race and in the cold water where the body gets cold and tired.

▼ You have to be able to use both double and single paddles and it doesn't hurt to practise with a clunky old paddle because in some races you have to use what the organisers give you, not your beautiful new racing paddle.

▼ If you're thinking of the Raid Gauloises, you'll need to practise with three in a Canadian canoe because they have a three/two combination in inflatables.

▼ It is very important to be water craft specific in your training because there are subtle changes in seating positions that become major changes after hours in the water. Double kayaks are wider than singles and you have to adjust your paddling technique to suit. Training in Canadian canoe isn't really a suitable simulation for rafting technique as the seating angle is significantly different and you're higher above the water. There's enough difference to make training in a raft a good idea, even if you can only do it in flat water. It is good to practise team co-ordination and get used to changing sides every 10 minutes or so to avoid straining one particular group of muscles. Of course, training in Canadians will supplement the occasional rafting session.

▼ You should also practise night paddling, not just in flat water but out in the ocean and on easy, moving water where a Grade 1 rapid can sound like a ferocious waterfall when you can't actually see what's coming up. So, it's a good idea to get used to the feeling and the noises, they're quite different at night. Please be safe though!

▼ In any sort of water craft, if the water conditions and wind are favourable, you'll want to be using a tent fly as a sail so practise that in training. In single kayaks you can raft up side by side and hold the sail up, the same for double kayaks, and if you've ever paddled a raft on flat water, you'll be looking for all the help you can get.

Water craft technique

Efficient technique in any kind of water craft can translate into hours saved, not to mention the advantage of preventing injury. I've seen beginners wasting so much energy on inefficient technique it's worth describing the proper technique here. Of all the sports included in adventure races, it is often paddling which seems to be the most neglected. It is probably one of the sports that takes the most effort to become proficient, as well. But if you're prepared to put in the time, a lot of gains can be made.

The lack of ability relative to cycling and running is probably related to the number of swim triathletes that come into the sport and the relative difficulty of accessing kayaks and kayaking.

Money invested in a coach is money well spent. However, a few basics for efficient technique are:

▼ Commonly now we use wing blades which are light, strong and efficient. But there's nothing wrong with using the basic tear drop or Italia style if you prefer.

▼ Stand the paddle upright and your outstretched hand should curl over at the first knuckle. This is a general rule of thumb for the right length although you can go a little longer if you're reasonably strong.

▼ The most efficient grip position is when your elbows are at right angles with the paddle held across the top of your head.

▼ Your right hand stays gripped on the paddle and the left hand feathers. Feathering is when the blades are offset, ideally at 70-80 degrees.

Beginners are easily spotted as the ones with bent arms and not using their torsos much. An efficient stroke begins with the blade entering the water as far forward as comfortably possible. So:

▼ Your forward arm needs to be fully extended;

▼ Elbow straight;

▼ And shoulder rotated fully forward (you may feel a bit like a wound up spring).

▼ Immerse the blade fully before you start pulling back (or before the spring starts unwinding);

▼ The strongest, most useful and most important part of the stroke is the first half, until the blade is about level with your knees.

Good posture in the boat is essential for the long hours you're going to spend in training and racing. You have to avoid slouching and sit up with a straight spine and with a slight forward lean. This will protect you and your back and give you good torso or spinal rotation. The vertebrae in your back need to be on top of each other to rotate, they can't turn when you're slouched. You can easily visualise this need for vertical alignment.

Efficient paddling does not just use the upper body. Good technique uses the powerful muscles of the legs, torso and shoulders in addition to the arms. Using your legs may sound a strange concept but what they actually do is help your backside swivel on the seat. If you like, this is the foundation for your upper body and the extra few degrees add immensely to the movement of the blade through the water (if you have a look at an Olympic K-1 boat you'll find a tiny, highly polished seat that lets the paddler swivel more easily and gain those extra centimetres).

A very common paddling injury is tendinitis, usually of the right wrist. The principal cause is usually insufficient endurance training for the event, exacerbated by too tight a grip on the shaft. The constant rotating of the right wrist to feather the blades correctly leads to overuse of that one, particular tendon. Sometimes, too, the paddle you use in the race has blades offset more than you've trained with and this additional rotation can cause the problem.

To avoid tendinitis, you have to follow the golden rule and build up slowly to the duration you expect to paddle in the race. Second, feather the paddle 70 degrees or 80 degrees rather than 90 degrees. Third, don't grip so hard. As you push the arm forward, release the pinkie (fourth and fifth) fingers so the wrist does not have to be cocked so tightly. And finally, a smaller diameter shaft may mean less stress on that wrist.

Tendinitis can also be aggravated by an incorrect grip in mountain biking. You need to keep your wrists straight, not bent, especially on the downhills.

Biking

The most notable feature about mountain biking in adventure races is that it is invariably quite long, goes up many long, steep hills and you always end up riding through the night which makes it seem even longer.

Another notable memory is that I usually end up with a very sore bum! How do you deal with this? I don't know. I have thought of putting sandpaper in my pants and finishing the session by hitting myself 100 times with a hammer to simulate how it might feel in the Southern Traverse. Certainly, it won't feel worse!

▼ One of the causes, I think, is that when racing you're wearing a pack and the extra weight makes the difference so the obvious solution is to train carrying a pack.

▼ Train on long, hard hills. I think it's important to do as much of your biking as possible on hills to build up good quads, strong legs.

▼ SPD — clip-in — pedals are very worthwhile and practise pedalling in 'circles', that is, pull up as well as pushing down. Using a wind trainer up to three times a week is a good exercise. Wind (or stationary) trainers work so well, if you can tolerate the boredom, because they are very 'honest,' there is no coasting downhill. They also promote good technique as you can tell by the 'whizz' sound if you are pedalling with an even pressure through the entire rotation. An hour on the wind trainer is equal to one and a half to two hours on the track.

▼ Ride on a variety of surfaces. Often in these races you'll find yourself on loosely gravelled roads which seem a bit like marbles under your tires. This is usually made worse because you have high pressure in the tires to lessen rolling resistance so make sure you simulate this in training, too.

▼ Riding on roads gives you a chance to bunch ride or even draft each other so that is something else to practise. It can be a good idea to join a local cycle club to get the experience in racing and bunch riding.

▼ It is important to have good posture. Hours of biking will give you sore shoulders and a sore back with an incorrect riding position. I'd recommend keeping your neck extended, head up and back straight and no hunching anywhere. Occasionally rise up out of the saddle to stretch your back, arms, hamstrings and legs.

▼ Try and ride with straight wrists, especially downhill, letting your elbows take the shocks. Sore wrists can exacerbate tendinitis beginning in paddling.

▼ Downhilling is very worthwhile to practise in training. Timidity can cost many minutes and a crash could mean the end of the race. Keep your weight back, even behind the seat if it's very steep, look ahead, planning your route well in advance, brake with a mix of front and rear and practise, practise, practise.

▼ Night riding is something that can't be avoided and can be fun but it deserves a lot of attention in training. Riding at night is very similar to riding downhill in that the further ahead you can see and plan, the faster you're going to be. Bright lights can increase speed by up to 20km/h!

▼ You can get these powerful lights at a bike shop. We've found a 12 watt halogen to be a good compromise between power and longevity of battery life. There are new bulbs using new technologies coming out, however. At present they are expensive but they will come down in price so keep an eye out for them as they'll use less battery.

▼ You might be able to use normal lights for easy riding and halogens for gnarly bits and downhills. On the road, you can use a combination of normal and halogen at the front if you keep together as a team, a more efficient use of lights and batteries, thus saving weight.

▼ Some bike shops and clubs run night races and I recommend

them. As in running, boring old rides become quite different and challenging at night.

Because bike stages tend to be long, it is important to have your bike set up properly. Your local bike shop can help with this. There are many occasions when my own bike or that of one of my team mates hasn't been set up quite properly and we've had to push when I've felt we should have been able to ride, saving energy and time. That's partly due to insufficient training and partly because the bike hasn't been properly set up.

▼ Check your seat height. For long hours of non-technical riding you'll need it about the same as for a road bike. A rule of thumb method is to put the arch of the foot on the pedal at the bottom of its stroke and you should be able to just straighten your knee.

▼ If you're doing gnarly single track that tests your balance and perhaps for downhill, you may want to lower your seat a centimetre or two. This will lower your centre of gravity and make it easier to get the feet on the ground for stability. I'd recommend you mark with a scriber or sharp screwdriver the ideal height of your saddle so its easy to reset. Having the seat at the right height will save stress on your quadriceps and strain on your back.

▼ Forward reach is important. In the normal riding position, the handlebar is usually between 3 and 10 cms in front of the line of sight to your front axle.

▼ Front suspension is worthwhile. Full suspension might seem like a good idea, it does give a plusher ride, but the weight penalty is too great after three or four hours — unless you've got deep enough pockets to buy the very high end, lightweight models.

▼ A trip to your bike shop is an investment that pays dividends in more comfortable riding, fewer chances of injury and faster times.

Mountaineering and rope skills

The Southern Traverse tends not to have the serious mountaineering sections that sometimes occur in the Raid and EcoChallenge. However, in all adventure races you will need to have a knowledge of snow and ice travel. All races also have sections where rope skills — including ascending or jumaring, abseiling or rappelling and safety ropes — are required.

Typically, there will be long, spectacular abseils and some particularly treacherous sections of the course may have ropes for safe travel which will require you to have harnesses and three points of contact, two on at all times and the third to transfer past an anchor or barrier.

Rope skills you can get at your local climbing wall but for full training, especially to prepare for snow and ice travel, it is a good idea to hire a registered mountain guide or someone from the Mountain Safety Council for a lesson.

The technique is very important. If you're blasé about it now and don't think it's very important, believe me, it will be when you come to need it on the race course.

The races always have a spectacular rope skills section somewhere. Height is involved and so your confidence with heights will be important — and perhaps sorely tested. Practice is the key to this — in all weathers and at night, too. It can be as simple as a rope from a tree, a balcony or, better, at your local climbing wall where there's good safety available and knowledge of the skills required. Remember to always practise with two points of contact at all times, with the third for transfers.

I find it a common misconception that once you've learned the basic procedures for two points of contact for safety, you know it all and don't need to practise. Practice is important for two main reasons, first for safety and second for speed. Ask yourself, "What if it's exposed, we haven't slept for three nights, there's a gale, it's night and pouring with rain?" But it is fun to practise and team co-ordination can save valuable minutes during the race (and sometimes hours at an impasse).

Taking up rock climbing is a fun way to practise, especially on a fixed rope, climbing up and then abseiling down. Be specific and wear a helmet and pack as you will in the race. Your centre of gravity and balance are markedly affected.

Respect your gear, look after it and DON'T tread on the rope. Double check each other's harnesses and knots and remember safety is paramount.

It is beyond the scope of this book to instruct you in alpine climbing, employ a registered guide or other qualified person for that. But there are a number of skills you'll need to learn. They include:

▼ The use of an ice axe, including self arrest;

▼ Kicking and cutting steps;

▼ Use of crampons and their adjustment (can you do this at night, on the snow, in a storm with frozen fingers?). A skifield is great place to practise;

▼ You'll need to know how to rope up for glacier travel;

▼ Knowing how to identify crevasses, seracs and other hazards;

▼ Knowing how to carry out a glacier rescue;

▼ Belaying and the use of ice screws;

▼ Avalanche hazard assessment, avalanche rescue and the use of an avalanche transceiver;

▼ Navigation in a white-out;

▼ Use of a Tyrolean traverse as it appears in many races today.

Miscellaneous

One of the wonderful things about overseas adventure races is they're tailored to suit the country and terrain they're held in, a very exciting aspect. To this end, extra events or disciplines may be introduced as they invariably add to the flavour. Examples include:

▼ Caving;

▼ Horse riding;

▼ Camel riding;

▼ Sailing;

▼ Skydiving;

▼ Parasailing;

▼ Diving.

As with all the other disciplines we've talked about, it is important to train specifically for and simulate as closely as possible the race situation. Although these sports may be out of your normal experience, and the required toys might not be in your toy box, it is important to make the effort to practise them.

Practise together as a team if possible and, as always, work into these new sports gradually or injury will occur. A good example is horses. Not many of us own a horse but you can go horse trekking together. Ring around to find the liveliest horses and an operator more open to innovation. Avoid the placid, 'nose-to-tail' treks as you need to learn to control livelier horses. I'd recommend an hour to start and a minimum of five sessions, up to 20, before the race.

Some of these sports may be difficult to practise, like, say rafting. But it is important to get out on the river at least once before the event. Or you can simulate white water in the ocean waves.

You can't expect to do well on race day without practice and the more practice, the better you'll be.

Good luck!

Big pictures

By Steve Gurney

Planning needs to start with a step backwards. Think about your family and the goals and values you have within it. What about your career? What are your long term prospects and desires? Where do you want to be in 5, 10 or 20 years time? This is the Big Picture, the reality, where planning begins.

Now you can move on to adventure racing and there are a few important questions to ask yourself here, too.

▼ Why are you doing this? Why are you planning an adventure race? What do you expect to get from it?

▼ What aspirations do you have as far as placing goes? Are you planning on just surviving to finish or do you want to be a major place-getter?

▼ Critically, does this goal of adventure racing fit in with the other areas of your life — family, work and other recreation — and do you have the support and co-operation of friends, family and workmates to fit in with these other areas because if they clash, you can be sure they will clash disastrously. You need to be sure all aspects support each other. You need to share your goals with the people who are important in your life and have their support and enthusiasm, too.

▼ And finally, are you being realistic? Is it realistic to expect to reach this high level of competition within the time schedule you've allowed?

You must ask yourself these questions because you must be under no misconception, have no misapprehensions — adventure racing and its training are very demanding. You need to allocate quite a lot of time because endurance training is be definition a lengthy process.

Don't get me wrong. It can be exciting and the time spent is well worth it if you're looking for excitement.

So, to get that big picture, write down your goals and aspirations and the placing you hope to get and then make up a programme, a calendar. You can make this as a spreadsheet on your computer, you can draw it up yourself, you can use a year planner or even a calendar on the wall.

Mark on your planner all the commitments you already have for the year, including any other races you want to do and there should be local races you want to incorporate. Mark in the family holidays, Christmas, Easter, work conferences, the annual fishing trip, anything that will impinge on your ability to go training. You have to co-ordinate them all. Don't try and rule over them, pretend they don't matter. You have to work with them.

Now let's look at the periodisation chart. It, too, is divided into 52 columns, each representing a week, with the known commitments clearly marked, periods where you know you're not going to be able to undertake your normal training. Conversely, you should also mark periods where you know you'll be able to do extra training.

Periodisation can be defined as dividing the year into phases or periods. Early in the year, for example, say 12 to 6 months before the chosen event, you'll need to be doing base training, essentially weekend trips. The pace will be slow and easy but the trips do need to be long to build up your endurance.

It is also important to use the periodisation chart to plan when you're going to develop your skills, when you're going to have lessons in horse riding, snow and ice climbing and so on. Snow training, obviously, needs to be done in winter or early spring and white water skills are more comfortably learned in the warmer months of summer.

Figure 1

PERIODISATION

COMPONENTS & TRAINING	Dec	Jan	Feb	March	April
					27 3 10 17 24
Calendar		Xmas hol		Family hol	Work conference
Intensity graph					
Phases		BASE & ENDURANCE			
Technique		Trail / Running / Hiking / Foot / Mtb / Horse			
		Outdoor Climbing			
		Whitewater Skills (Summer)			

SAMPLE

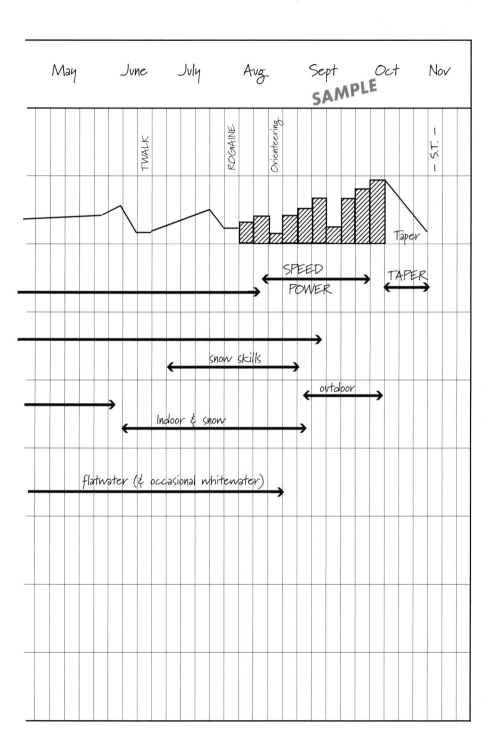

Periodisation is all about planning your year so it culminates in or peaks for the race you have chosen. Of course, you can — and should — have other races you want to do through the year leading up to the main event. You should include these and plan how to do 'mini-peaks' for them.

Along one axis of the graph (Figure 1) you'll have columns representing weeks. For the other axis, divide the training into its components:

Intensity indicates how intense your training should be in any particular week. Endurance needs to be developed months (or even years) out from the race so it needs to be periodised early on. Strength needs to be developed early in the periodisation, in the form of steady hill training, heavy packs and possibly weights at the gym. Speed is relatively low in priority for adventure racing but is useful as a method of developing power. This need only be done later in the periodisation. Strength is a prerequisite for power. Broadly speaking, power is a product of strength with speed.

Technique shows where you've planned that component for each of your disciplines. You'll want to look at when you're going to do your water skills, what phase of the year, when you're going to learn your mountaineering skills, when you'll work on your biking, abseiling and so on.

About five or six months before the Southern Traverse, or whatever event you're working towards, assuming that you have a base of long, slow distance, you'll be ready to pick up the intensity a little and perhaps do more hills. Start working just a little bit harder for six or eight weeks until around three months before the race. At this stage, start being specific in the type of training you're doing.

It should simulate the race as closely as possible. You'll have a bit more of an idea what's in the race from the newsletters

American Dave Horne being brought in at gun point — first Coast to Coast

Checking mandatory gear

Right: Be an adventure racer, see the world — Raid Gauloises, Papagonia

How not to kayak

Right: Steve Gurney (left) and John Howard check the route

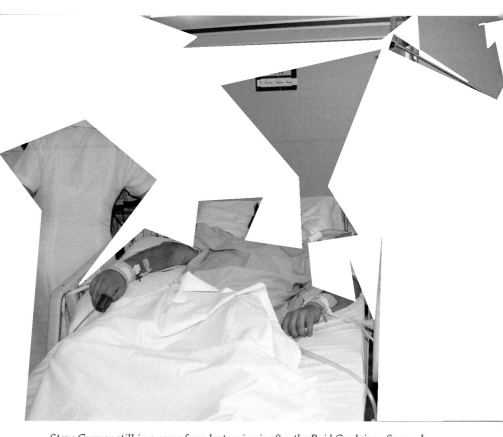

Steve Gurney still in a coma from leptospirosis after the Raid Gauloises, Sarawak

Team with the locals for local support and media attention — John Howard and Steve Gurney, Sarawak

Over: Nevis Valley, Southern Traverse

that have been sent out to you. You'll tailor and fine tune your training a little and become a bit more intense with more specific sessions. I'd also encourage another, finer aspect of periodisation here, where you have two or three hard weeks followed by an easy recovery week then another two or three weeks just a little bit harder than the previous hard weeks with another period of recovery after that. And then comes a final two or three weeks where the training is even harder again, just before your three week taper down to the race.

The taper should not be a sudden stop in training. It needs to be a gradual decrease in duration and a slight increase in intensity so instead of going for an hour's run, you might go for 40 minutes with some hill sprints or faster sessions in it. Instead of a hill bike ride for an hour and a half, you might just do some pick ups where you get your heart rate nice and high (above your anaerobic threshold. Anaerobic threshold for beginners is when you're too puffed to hold a conversation) for a few seconds and drop it back down again to recover for five minutes before getting it back up again for a few seconds and then back to 120 beats a minute for five minutes. Rotate through that sort of cycle five to eight times.

Equally essential as part of the taper, with the reduced duration and the increased intensity, is a vastly increased recovery period between sessions. The taper is just a sharpening phase.

Starting from the big picture, you've looked at the 'whys' (why do you want to do this and does it fit in with the other goals in your life?) and you've looked at a little more detail and the phases for the year.

From there, you can take one of those weeks on your racing chart and write a little training schedule for that period. You can work back into even more detail by taking one of the days from that week and figure out exactly what you're going to do that day and how it is going to fit into your diary, along with work, family and friends.

The big picture has been broken down into little bite-sized chunks so that the seemingly huge task of competing successfully in the Southern Traverse is now set before you in very achievable daily tasks.

We've included a sample weekly training schedule (Figure 2). You need to make up your own plan (copy our sample, if you like) and it is very important to allow plenty of time for recovery. For example, wait two or three days after a hard, hilly session carrying a heavy pack before you try anything like that again.

Recovery can be either a rest with stretching and massage or it can be something easy, like walking or even swimming at a moderate, easy pace just to help your muscles get back to normal. You don't want to do anything hard again until after you have allowed your body to recover and rebuild.

While it is not total rest, a good compromise is to balance your schedule with alternate sessions of upper body and lower body exercise, for example, kayaking one session and running the next day. Of course, your legs are used in the kayak so you don't want to do a really hard interval session if your legs are sore.

The example schedule shown here conforms to seven days but I actually prefer to work on a more open ended format. If my body hasn't recovered from a particular session I've scheduled, then I think it's important to allow time for recovery and put off the next hard session or do something easier, instead. It is essential to allow time for recovery because without it your training will be less effective or even detrimental.

Figure 2

	KAYAK	BIKE	FOOT	OTHER
MONDAY	Rough water practice 1 hr Moderate pace		Orienteering in forest 1½ hrs Moderate pace	
TUESDAY		Mtb 2hrs Moderate		
WEDNESDAY	Time trials 40–50 mins Hard pace		40 mins with pack Hills Moderate pace	
THURSDAY	Rough water practice Easy 40–60 mins	Windtrainer session 40mins Hard with intervals		
FRIDAY	— R E S T D A Y —			
SATURDAY	A Hiking/running trip 2 days B Sea kayak or whitewater trip 2 days C Sat orienteering Sun sea kayak			
SUNDAY	D Overnight (24hr) group rogaining E Mtb overnight trip – Sat 10hr Mtb Sun 4hr run			

All long sessions in the weekend Easy to Moderate pace but do not stop much. Make sessions continuous but easy pace.

It is important to listen to your body. It hurts or is sore for a reason.

The weekend sessions all have various options. One weekend you'll want to do a long, two day run or hike with an overnight. The next weekend you might do a white water trip with your team and the following weekend it will be different again.

The important thing is not to concentrate on just one discipline unless, of course, it is very weak. Rather, you should vary your outings so you get a good, all round experience. An essential component of the weekly schedule is that you do long sessions to simulate the race when you have time and that is usually in the weekends.

You also need some shorter sessions that are a little bit harder, to simulate the hills and speed of the race. You don't want to combine these components with your long sessions, however, because you'll get burned out. It's best to split your training into its components and make it enjoyable.

The hard sessions where you've got endurance combined with pace are best saved until race day.

Staying injury free

For adventure racers, there is, as they say, good news and bad news. The good news is that adventure racers and multisporters tend to suffer fewer injuries than single sport athletes. The bad news is they still get injured but usually less severely.

The main reason for fewer injuries seems to be the cross-training aspects in preparation for racing. In other words, balancing muscle groups are also trained. Just the same, the common injuries remain in the shins and ankles in running, knees from cycling and paddling affects the shoulders and lumbar region.

"Muscles and tendons get overused for a number of reasons," says sports physiotherapist and dedicated multisporter Glenn Muirhead. "It is usually just due to a weakness or imbalance somewhere around the body." It is the balancing of the muscle group development, built up through training for the various disciplines, that has reduced the incidence of these typical injuries among adventure racers. This also allows an easier physical and more psychologically beneficial recovery because, for example, if you roll an ankle, you're off running for two weeks but you can still paddle a kayak or ride a bike. Training doesn't have to stop and fitness need not be affected.

But how do you go about treatment for a chronic, classic overuse injury like an Achilles tendon strain? Understanding the pathology of the problem is crucial and to this end a training diary can help. This will let whoever is treating you know what level of training you're at, how often you're running each week and for how long (it will also help you spot patterns and analyse problems). Then they have to find the level of dysfunction. Is it worst first thing in the morning? How sore does it get when you run? Does it stop you running? Is it getting better or worse?

Only then can the clinical decisions be made. As adventure racers, you are usually accustomed to goals set in training, so it makes it easier for you to adjust to goals set in a recovery programme. You will usually find it easier psychologically to know that even if the injury is still sore in two weeks, it will definitely be getting better in four weeks. But you must also take into account where you'll be running. After a time, the Achilles might last for 20km of flat running, the direct distance indicated on a map for the running section of an adventure race, for example, but it certainly won't hold up for 30km of leaping from rock to rock, which might well be the true distance and underfoot conditions of that section.

Prevention, of course, is always better than cure, so how can you minimise the chances of injury? There are a few basics to begin with.

Some of the very best athletes visit their sports medicine specialist every few months, certainly at the end of an off season and the beginning of a new period of intense training. They go through a complete biomechanical analysis, including exercises and stretches, which looks at strength, flexibility, muscle endurance and power. It is primarily designed to try and pick up any problems that may occur later as the volume of training intensifies. It is particularly useful if there is a history of injury in any particular area.

Let's go back to that Achilles. The flexibility and strength of the calf muscle are tested and the mobility around the ankle and the joints in the foot is looked at. Then it's on to the treadmill to check the way you run and finally the strength through the hip and pelvis are checked. "A lot of advance has been made in the last five years in pelvic stability," says Muirhead. "That has helped a lot of small, niggling injuries."

A biomechanical analysis is the ideal but is it for everyone? Even if you run in the middle or the back of the pack it can help.

If you find you're getting regular injuries, however minor, during training you will certainly benefit. It can be a hard call and seem like a lot of unjustified expense. In the long term, however, it may well save you money, time and stress by getting you into the right shoes, with or without orthotics, and directing the specialist to exercises and therapies that will correct other problems and thus reduce or prevent later injury.

Even then, you have to remember to start every exercise period slowly and build up, whether running, cycling or paddling. Few sports specialists these days recommend stretching before exercise, preferring it to be done when warm or for time to be set aside every day. The benefit of stretching is not in question, just the timing. The one exception is if you have a predisposing injury. Then stretching of that particular area before exercise may be called for.

If you have a history of a particular injury or are concerned about a particular injury, to ankles or knees, for example, learn good strapping technique. This will also have psychological benefits by reducing worry and stress.

And, of course, proper technique is essential. It doesn't matter what the discipline, good technique will make you more efficient, faster, use less energy, increase your endurance and minimise injury. Good technique is an important part of injury prevention.

Renowned sports medicine specialist Dr Ruth Highet also acknowledges that adventure racers suffer relatively fewer injuries. Her concerns, whether in endurance training or during an adventure race itself, are particularly in the area she refers to as "environmental conditions."

Top of the list is hypothermia, a problem exacerbated by the races typically traversing mountainous regions and descending or crossing rivers. Mountain weather is famous for it's changeability. This means not only rapid fluctuations in temperature, invariably downwards when you can least afford that, but also strong winds and rain, changing to snow as the temperature drops — perfect hypothermia conditions for the inadequately clothed and poorly fed. These conditions are so often made worse, sadly, by the athlete's superior fitness which, in this case, means lack of body fat and hence insulation.

The same is true on the water. Wet clothes and bodies conduct heat away much faster, lowering the core temperature. Add in total immersion, which also increases fatigue, further lowering the body's defences, and hypothermia is a constant fear.

What can be done? Plenty. For a start, appropriate clothing is essential. There are many synthetics today that stop wind and water, stay warm when wet and dry quickly. Remember, too, that a race director's "Minimum gear requirements" is just that — a minimum. It is designed for survival, not comfort. An extra, dry, lightweight layer, with little bulk or weight, stored at the bottom of your pack, just might keep you or a team-mate in the race.

And, of course, the effects of hypothermia are felt faster and worse when you are tired, undernourished and dehydrated. Fuel — food — and fluid are essential not just to keep the body moving but to help it stay warm and healthy.

Cold muscles also have less stretch, leading more easily to muscle strain and decreased flexibility. It is important to keep working on flexibility through the race. Don't just stop to rest, spend a few minutes stretching, too. You'll easily make up any 'lost' time through increased mobility, agility and balance.

As fatigue increases in any endurance event, there is an increased risk of musculo-skeletal injury. Minor sprains or strains become more common and the chance of a fracture increases. A particular problem associated with fatigue and cold is eccentric muscle stress, over-extending muscles. Running downhill is a classic example but you can work on this during training and reduce the risk of such an injury.

The importance of team-mates cannot be overemphasised. This is where good team dynamics and communication come into play. It is invariably team-mates who will notice the signs of hypothermia, usually long before, if ever, you will. They'll notice balance and agility problems, for example, and take appropriate action before real problems develop.

Recent research has also provided an indicator of muscle damage. Muscle enzymes are normally retained within the tissue but move into the blood stream during prolonged exercise and injury. Blood samples taken through any endurance event will show an ever increasing enzyme count. Here again, proper training, technique and nutrition all go to lessening the damage. It can take 10-15 days before enzyme levels return to normal.

It has also been found that muscle adaptation requires some initial damage — and release of enzymes — before the repair, and strengthening, can begin.

Over-training is another area of major concern for Dr Highet. Periods of rest are an integral part of any training regime, allowing muscle recovery before the next phase begins. A period of rest before the event is also crucial and, in fact, many athletes have turned in their best performances after a slight illness, for example, has forced a halt to all training a few days before the event. It is important to begin the race, and, for that matter, any training, feeling fresh and rested.

The symptoms of over-training are clear, if not to you then to your team-mates, friends and family. Typically, they include an increased incidence of infections in the upper respiratory tract.

This seems to be because of a reduced level of immunological defence. There is general irritability and tiredness, coupled with sleep problems (you can learn to sleep. Hypnotherapists, for example, have had great success here). You lose appetite, don't eat and may even have feelings of nausea. And you'll have constantly sore muscles.

The solution? Cut back on training and get plenty of rest.

The taking of anti-inflammatories and painkillers during a race is, for many athletes, a vexed question. The medical advice is quite simple — don't! The pain is there for a reason. You can't expect to mask the symptoms without making the cause worse. The risks of more severe injury are too high. A recognised side-effect of anti-inflammatories is gastro-intestinal bleeding and any symptoms of dehydration can make this worse. Strapping and pressure bandaging, done properly, are more likely to be immediately effective, more useful and less harmful in the long term.

And if you want a painkiller for a headache, are you sure it hasn't been brought on by dehydration? If you do, ultimately, feel the need for a painkiller, paracetamol, says Dr Highet, is the most benign. Perhaps that should be rephrased — is the least likely to cause real harm.

It's worth mentioning oral hygiene here. For some people it is never an issue, many others report mouth ulcers and teeth problems. The cause is usually the consumption of sports drinks and the like, especially when sucked in regular, small sips from a hydration bladder system. Regular tooth brushing in transitions helps and so does gargling with saline solutions — an uncomfortable and at times painful problem with a simple solution.

Feet

Whole books have been written on feet and foot-care. Badly blistered feet have cost races.

Every racer seems to have a favourite barrier cream or coating. What works for one won't necessarily work for you. Some sports medicos aren't even convinced of the need for any.

What they do say, though, is that socks are just as important as the shoes. There's a bewildering array out there in a range of fabrics and yarns. The new synthetics or a mix of synthetic and wool seem to be the most popular. They need to wick moisture away from the foot as quickly as possible, to dry quickly and to reduce friction. Two thin socks are always better than one thick one. Don't try a new pair on race day, use them in training first to ensure they work properly for you.

Now, on to shoes themselves. Fit, obviously, is critical. Let's assume you've been to visit the sports podiatrist to have the biomechanics of your foot checked. Each shoe is different, make sure you get the right shoe to suit the biomechanics of your foot. Reducing pronation, for example, will reduce sliding — friction — and hence blisters. Some shoe specialists have a treadmill in the store and qualified technicians to check your biomechanics and help select the right shoe for you. Remember, they're your feet you're putting in the shoes and you have to train and race in them.

It helps, too, to have shoes that drain quickly, the more water around the foot, the more the chance of damage. Try shoes on in the afternoon when they've swollen up a bit and for the race, you'll need a pair at least half a size larger (some say a full size) than normal to allow for the inevitable swelling after days on your feet.

At the inaugural Elf Authentic Adventure in the Philippines, some 90 percent of racers suffered severe foot problems. They were so bad, the two lead teams, including John Howard, Ian Adamson and Cathy Sassin, fired off rescue flares. Head medical officer Dr Olivier Aubry said:

"There is a combination of problems. First, poor foot management from the race start, including racers choosing not to disinfect daily, not to change socks frequently enough and not to apply generous quantities of Vaseline or other greases ... Combined with biting ants and exotic plants, teams have arrived with feet cut, swollen and so tender the athletes cannot walk on them."

Note: Also available today are a range of homeopathic sports remedies. They can't stop blisters or sprains but they are designed to overcome sleep deprivation, reduce muscle soreness and speed recovery. Some racers swear by them.

Food for performance

Proper nutrition will ensure you perform at your best for longer and recover faster. It might not actually win you the race but bad nutrition will guarantee you lose it.

Good nutrition makes good sense. Some trainers have gone so far as to say that improvement in nutrition is the single biggest reason for improved performance in the last 10 years. Certainly any competitive athlete ignores it at his or her peril. It is right up there with specificity and skills training for multisporters — and all too often neglected.

Nutritionist Shona Jaray puts it this way: "There are a lot of athletes who suddenly realise, just a week or two before an event, that they'd better think about their nutrition. While that's good, better than not thinking about it at all, I can't help thinking, 'I wish you'd come to see me six months ago and I could have done a lot for you because [now] I'm having to guess what to do.'"

When an athlete comes to her, she says, she sits down and asks a lot of questions, both about the physical training and current eating habits. From this information she sets a basic guideline, an ideal nutrition regime, "but to get things person-perfect you have to tinker and [in just two weeks] I don't have time for that sort of tinkering."

Nutrition is important to adventure racers and multisporters simply because of the duration of the event and the hours and hours spent in training. Under a couple of hours and it is relatively simple to muddle your way nutritionally through most things. Beyond that duration, however, and problems start to arise. Early adventure racers found their way by trial and error, adopting and adapting methods from other endurance events. Modern nutrition has become a science that allows you to tailor a regime to your specific requirements — with fewer of the problems and disasters that overtook the pioneers. We're all different, however, and what works for one may not be exactly right for you.

Proper nutritional preparation will allow you to give a better performance, to sustain a higher rate for longer, and it will allow you to recover faster. And that, too, leads to greater enjoyment, which is, after all, what sport is all about.

Nutrition for triathlons, Ironman events and basic multisport activities is fairly well sorted these days. Adventure racing adds that wee bit extra, makes those few additional demands. It is tempting to say it is just an extension of multisport practice but that requirement for peak performance day after day requires special attention. If you don't get it right, says Jaray, you might not finish or you'll finish in very poor shape, perhaps by strength of will alone, mind over matter, forcing the body to keep moving.

When the event comes, you have to be entirely focused, planning several days ahead. It is imperative you get everything right, starting from Day 1 and on through Days 2, 3 and so on. If you don't eat properly on that first day, you'll be paying for it very quickly.

"You really have to plan to have adequate food and fuel," says Jaray, "and ensure you've got adequate electrolyte replacement."

There are all too many people who say they drink when they're thirsty and eat when they're feeling hungry. Or they might say they can't eat or drink while they're exercising. "The cold, hard facts are, you have to practise and you get used to it."

But for some people that's not easy. There are all sorts of practical ways, however, of addressing the problem of discomfort. "When I talk to people, I learn what they can tolerate. I question them more and more deeply until I learn perhaps they can take a sip or two of water. It's the keyhole, the crack I need. I then get them to do a little bit more and we start in little bits." When people say they can't run and drink, she gets them to just take a couple of sips every 5-10 minutes and build on that. "After six weeks your stomach no longer sounds like a washing machine."

Many of the top adventure racers have tried a variety of diets through their careers but without exception they've come back to normal diets, to eating regular food. "I'm glad to hear it," says Jaray, "I work on the principal of normal foods. I'm well known for not liking supplements."

Or as Ian Adamson, one of the world's top adventure racers and kayak marathon world record holder, puts it: "I maintain a balanced diet with sufficient calories to provide fuel for the physical training. I do not take supplements unless my diet lacks a particular nutrient but I believe strongly in eating the right foods, as defined by the recommended dietary allowances. In general, I am in tune enough with my body to know when I need a particular nutrient and then go and eat something rich in that food."

When Jaray begins working with someone, she starts first by trying to get a feel for their eating habits, looking at it first from the point of view of health, "you have to be healthy." Then she looks at the demands imposed by a particular sport. Finally she is able to begin making suggestions.

"If I do a plan for somebody, I base the plan on their current eating habits. If their current eating habit is a hamburger every day for lunch, we'll discuss that and find something else. If I don't think [their diet] is appropriate, we'll look at ways of changing it. I look at modifying what they currently do, rather than saying they have to eat this, this or this."

That makes sense. If you don't like the taste of the alternative food, it's not freely available or it's too expensive then the whole programme isn't going to work. And if some kind of special preparation is required, something that is different from anybody else in the household, that only makes the problem worse.

In the early days of nutrition, just a few years ago, charts and trainers talked about percentages, 60 percent of your calories coming from carbohydrates and up to 70 percent for really long endurance events. The theory was fine but if the athlete was only consuming 1500 calories a day, for example, that would be far from adequate. People laugh because it seems so obvious but there are documented cases, particularly of women, where the diet appears to be superbly balanced, it's just that it is woefully inadequate in terms of total calories for the amount of exercise undertaken. So, thankfully, that system no longer operates.

Now the system operates on so many grams of carbohydrate per kilogram of ideal bodyweight, taking into consideration the amount of training. If you're doing endurance training, you're going to need per day, 9-10 grams of carbohydrate per kilogram of your ideal bodyweight. And since endurance athletes have an even greater need for protein than body builders, you'll probably also need about $1^1/_2$ grams of protein per kilogram of ideal bodyweight.

So what happens during an event, during the Southern Traverse, for example? Research has shown that the muscles have the ability to take up no more than 60 grams of carbohydrate per hour.

"I'd make sure," says Jaray, "looking at it on an hour by hour basis, there was 60 grams of carbohydrate available per hour, from a mixture of food and fluid. And then, because the Southern Traverse is at least four days long, obviously we'd need some protein in there.

"With longer events, you tend to get the muscles using branch chain amino acids as fuel. The reason for that is not entirely clear but the possibility exists that this happens when the carbohydrate supply is low. It could just be wear and tear on the muscles and that tends to make them break down a bit. But for whatever reason, I would be looking very carefully at the protein intake for a multi-day event. I'd also be looking at the amount of fluid and making sure there was enough sodium being replaced so you didn't get into problems of hyponatremia."

Hyponatremia is not just a nasty name, it is a condition increasingly recognised as a potentially severe problem for endurance athletes. Also known as water intoxication, it is, simply, a sodium deficiency, caused by the flushing of sodium from the blood by the constant intake of water, exacerbated, especially in hot weather, by constant sweating. Symptoms include nausea and cramps in the early stages which can lead to the much more serious disorientation and low blood pressure. Fitting, a coma and even death are possible, even though the body is well hydrated.

The solution is to ensure there is adequate sodium in your drinks and food, although no ideal intake has yet been determined. Salt tablets are not recommended. Sprinkle salt on your food if you feel you need more. Sodium also helps the body to process any fluids consumed.

She would also have the athlete do a sweat test. She would send the individual off for a two or three hour training period, for example, and weigh them before and after the session, taking into account the amount of food and fluid consumed. As much as possible, the expected weather and temperature conditions should be simulated although this is extremely difficult for adventure racing. Because everybody sweats at a different rate, this is the best way to get a feel for how much each individual's fluid needs replacing every hour.

Remember, too, we're all different and while there will be broad similarities, all nutrition regimes need to be looked at on an individual basis.

Should supplements be used during an event? "Yes, absolutely!"

Supplements are also useful to have during training. If you're training for a few hours, on a long bike ride, for example, or kayaking, supplements represent an easy, safe and practical solution to the problem of maintaining calorie and carbohydrate levels. You can stuff them in your pocket. They don't get ruined if you sit on them or go black, squishy and revolting and because they're sealed they have a long shelf life. They're the ideal thing to have lying around in your pocket.

There is, however, one basic mistake that all too many people make. They consume their Leppin and keep going or else they wash it down with a sports drink "and really, for every Leppin-style supplement, you need at least 300 mils of water, plain water, with it."

The reason is simple. If you take a look at the basic information on sports drinks, you see that up to 8 percent carbohydrate will be absorbed as rapidly as or perhaps even faster than plain water. "Beyond 8 percent, you get delayed absorption. The stuff sits in your stomach and if it's very strong [combined Leppin and sports drink, for example] you may well get water coming back into the stomach to dilute the mixture so it can be absorbed. Now, exercise is very different from being at rest so that if you're exercising intensely, you have to give that Leppin every chance of being absorbed. If it sits in your stomach and draws fluid in, that is a major cause of gut cramp and nausea while exercising."

Jaray recounts the experience of having spoken to many people, especially those who have done the Ironman, who complain of having taken Leppins and then feeling sick. "Did you take water with it?" "No, I washed it down with sports drink to give me some more energy."

So is it a question of either a Leppin-style supplement or a sports drink? Sort of, seems to be the simple answer. During a long event or even on a long training session, you can get bored consuming the same thing the whole time. If you're out on a long bike ride, for example, leave home with the drink bottles full of sports drinks. When you've finished those, stop off at a garage and refill them with plain water. Then you can have your Leppin and water combination — and a change in taste. Besides, it's a hassle and can be very messy to carry powder to mix up a new lot of drink.

Supplements and sports drinks are equally good, it's a matter of taste and convenience.

However, there are some drinks that have come on the market recently that are not suitable for consumption during endurance training or competition. Touted as 'energy drinks', like V and Red Bull, Jaray believes they're not suitable for endurance training "because their carbohydrate (CHO) is probably over 20 percent and they have caffeine in them. Although, when you're exercising, caffeine doesn't work as a diuretic, I still think they're not suitable because of their high CHO content."

Lucozade is another product that appears to cause some confusion. It is often promoted as a sports drink and it is fine as a carbohydrate replacement after exercise but does not work as well as a fluid and energy replacement sports drink during training because it has a high CHO content of around 23-25 percent.

But that still leaves plenty to choose from. There is a huge number of fluid and energy replacement sports drinks on the market now and "the right one for you is the one you like the taste of, the one that's available and suits your pocket. They've all got slightly different formulations." VitaSport by Hansells, for example, has one of the highest sodium contents and that is important for adventure racers because it replaces some of the sodium lost during exercise. It is also one of the cheapest but if you don't like it, it's not the one for you. Jaray actually did the specifications for that particular drink "so I know it's good and it's cheap!"

It is important to establish well before an event exactly what sports drink and/or supplement you're going to use. You have to like the taste and then you'll have more. And if, for example, the race organisers provide a special drink during the event, you have to practise using that drink in training so you know exactly how it will affect you.

Protein is the basis of our muscle and tissue and part of the blood, hormones, enzymes and so on. It can also be used as fuel by the body if all the carbohydrate is used up so if there is insufficient protein in your diet, it is very likely you'll end up with muscle wasting. "This is on the bottom end of the scale and it is absolutely appalling." The same problem can occur if the total calorie intake is completely inadequate.

You need protein for muscle building and maintenance. There is a body of research that shows, too, that a small amount of protein added in with the carbohydrate after training will lead to even faster and better recovery. That doesn't mean you should take a protein supplement. Rather, a bowl of cereal with milk will provide sufficient protein, or a chicken and salad roll.

And make sure you get plenty of rest.

Saving weight

Equipment for adventure racing can be summed up in two words — 'light' and 'tough.' Of the two, tough is the more important because there's no point in having the latest, lightest, most exotic, most beautiful, most functional and most expensive toy if it breaks the first time you try to use it.

Nor can you take the manufacturer's word about it either, be it for carabiner or kayak, backpack or bicycle. You have to test it yourself in conditions similar to a race environment and be thoroughly comfortable with using it.

And, of course, reality, in the form of your budget, comes into it, too. You want the lightest and strongest you can afford. Adventure racing, including its multisport guise, is growing at such a phenomenal rate that many manufacturers are now designing specialist equipment for it.

In some races, Race Directors are now providing equipment for certain sections, boats, bicycles and even in-line skates, for example. This at least ensures nobody is disadvantaged (or maybe that everybody is disadvantaged equally) by having relatively inferior gear. You still need to train, however, and more often that not you'll race with your own bike if not kayak, because of the problems of international transport.

Mountain bike

Way up at the extreme end are titanium, carbon fibre and other exotic alloys and plastics. But most of us can't afford toys like these and have to be more realistic. It is important, though, to buy the best you can afford, especially the components as they'll usually break or malfunction long before the frame.

Should you get a bike with full suspension? Certainly it will give you a more comfortable ride but after three or four hours you'll be paying the penalty of greater weight and reduced efficiency. Unless, of course, those super exotic, fantastically lightweight goodies are within your budget. Front shocks only are a safer compromise that will still give you improved handling, especially downhill, without the weight penalty and increased complexity with its attendant maintenance problems.

Another weight saver that will dramatically increase efficiency is SPD or click-in pedals. They let you 'pedal in circles' to let you pedal further, faster and with less energy.

You can be sure of one thing, if a vital piece of equipment — derailleur, gear movement, rim, whatever — is going to break (and it will), it will do so at the worst possible moment. It is one of those immutable laws. It is essential you've had a few hours under race-type conditions with any new purchases and that you have the tools to fix problems and know how to use them.

Remember to talk over your requirements thoroughly with the retailer and get them to set seat height and position and handlebar reach to your optimum settings (see the chapter on Fitness, Skills and Training for rule of thumb settings).

Kayak

Don't over-reach yourself here. Sure, an Evolution is a super fast boat and maybe you can paddle it on flat, calm water, in the evenings when the wind has dropped, during training. Can you still do it when you're exhausted, the wind picks up and the waves are over a metre high? Or down a Grade 2 rapid? An Evolution upside down is very slow and your health and fitness are endangered.

So be practical. A sensible alternative is a sea kayak. It will handle any conditions likely to be faced in a race with great equanimity. There is also some movement towards four-person teams in adventure racing which should be taken into consideration. Two-person kayaks could well become the boat of choice with a still tentative suggested minimum width of 55cm (50cm for single-seaters) — width equals stability. Anyway, it is to your advantage to train with a partner and you have the added benefit of having someone to talk to, a real boon during those long training sessions.

Make sure the paddle is the right length and shape for your level of skill. Longer paddles require extra strength and technique and are something you may eventually work up to. In the meantime, stick to the rule of thumb — with the paddle upright, your upstretched hand should curl over the end at the first knuckle.

Personal gear

A number of manufacturers, including some major international names, have woken up to the fact there is a rapidly growing demand and are making products specifically for adventure racing.

Let's start with clothing. Hats and gloves are vital, windproof at least and quick drying. On the body, layering is the only way to go. The new synthetics are amazing in their ability to wick moisture away from the body, keep you warm even when wet and dry quickly. Some resist (body) odours better than others. In fact, new, lightweight, itchless woollen undershirts are proving popular among endurance athletes, not least because of their ability to minimise odours (your team-mates, friends and family might thank you even if you can't smell the difference).

The top layer needs to be highly breathable, windproof and waterproof. Depending on conditions, that can range from a new, lightweight, fold-away-to-nothing jacket and pants that are windproof but will keep out a shower to heavy duty parkas and overpants that will keep out waterfalls and blizzards.

The right combination will not only let you race to the best of your ability, it will also keep you warm, healthy — and alive.

The ever-pressing question is what do you wear on your feet? Start with socks and already the choice is confusing. There are many variations of combinations of synthetic fibres and wool is making a major comeback in mixes with synthetics. They need to minimise friction, dry quickly and keep your feet warm when required. Try them out first in training. Are your feet still blister free? What about after 12 hours or 24? Dry, clean socks go a long way to providing comfortable, healthy feet.

When it comes to shoes, a biomechanical check is a great way to start to ensure you get the type of shoe that is right for you. Do you pronate, supinate or is your foot plant neutral? Most of us are pronators or neutral but many shoe stores have trained assistants and treadmills to confirm your running style and help select the appropriate shoe. Try several different shoes, take your time and remember comfort and fit are paramount. It is also better to try shoes in the afternoon when your feet have enlarged slightly and still go up a half to a full size to allow for the more dramatic swelling that comes from extended exercise periods and actual races. Shoes that are too small are guaranteed to cause blisters and black nails.

Shoes are, in many respects, one of mankind's most damaging inventions. They enclose and restrict the foot and enfeeble natural muscular and skeletal movement, leading to a whole raft of injuries, not just in the foot. Barefooted runners have a completely unrestricted foot action and seldom seem to suffer injuries. Very recently, major sports shoe manufacturers, led by Adidas, have recognised the benefits of allowing the shoes to mimic the natural movement of the foot as closely as possible. Reports already suggest there are fewer injuries among athletes wearing shoes like this.

As more people have taken up adventure racing and others have switched their training from roads to off-road tracks and in the hills, so, too, have the manufacturers responded. One leading sports shoe maker has even sent out an international directive that off-road and trail running shoes should make up 25 percent of sales. That mark hasn't been reached anywhere yet but just a very few years ago this category didn't even exist.

Increasingly, shoes are being purpose built for adventure racing. They come from two directions. Established sports shoe companies are providing tougher, more stable products and boot makers are using their skills and technology to build lightweight footwear suitable for the new sport. These new-style shoes are light and strong, built to withstand the punishment of regular soaking, constant wear, bogs, boulders, ice, sand, roads and rocks that would see a pair of regular running shoes quickly consigned to the trash can — if there were one available out there in the wilderness.

And remember, wear them a few times before you race in them.

The other item of major concern is what you carry your extra clothing, equipment and food in — your back pack. These, too, have changed radically in the last few years, driven by the demands of adventure racers and other endurance athletes. As with so many things, you'll get what you pay for.

A cheap pack will usually be heavier, carry less, unable to expand, likely to fall to bits quickly and may well prove uncomfortable to wear after a few hours. The best packs have been carefully designed and tested to meet the needs of the most demanding adventure racers. They're light, of course, and made of tough new materials. They're expandable, too, to take loads for several days and, conversely, they can be cinched up tight to stop smaller, lighter loads from flopping around. They also have pockets and places for all your extra paraphernalia, from ice axes down to squeezies for CHO replacement.

So many things are getting lighter, stronger and more versatile. Go to your local climbing store and drool over the new lightweight goodies — ice axes, hammers, ice screws, snow anchors, jumars, descenders, carabiners. Head lamps are essential and getting lighter, stronger and simpler. Your watch can also be your compass and altimeter.

The rules for buying gear are really very simple. Buy the lightest, toughest equipment you can afford. And make sure you're familiar with it before you begin racing.

Plotting a course

Heinous: *1. Odious; highly criminal; infamous. 2. Grievous, severe. 3. Full of hate. 4. Term frequently used to describe a particularly unpleasant stage in the Southern Traverse —and other adventure races.*

Teams are the key to most adventure racing, to the extent that the term 'expedition racing' is beginning to gain currency. Even so, the most successful events seem to revolve round an individual. The Southern Traverse is no exception.

The individual in this instance is Geoff Hunt, a friendly, likeable man and a keen and tenacious competitor. It is this skill as a competitor that has led him to design courses for the racers.

National Geographic Explorer Channel host Boyd Matson, after his brutal introduction to adventure racing in the Southern Traverse, put it this way: "Some of these events are made for television. The Southern Traverse is a course for competitors. Keep it that way." And that's from a television show host!

But that is Geoff's plan. He can't afford to do anything else, anyway. He can't compete with the financial resources available to some of the other international events. He has to take a potential handicap and turn it into an attribute. But who is Geoff Hunt and why has he been able to bring his event to such international prominence, to be the third leg of that international adventure racing triumvirate?

When multisport began in New Zealand in 1980, Hunt was there, lining up with the likes of adventure racing legend John Howard. The driving force for those early events was the irrepressible Robin Judkins, these days irrevocably connected with the Coast to Coast. During the 1980 ski season, Judkins overheard talk of a weird American event that involved different outdoor sports. As is usually the case, reality was distorted somewhat, the distances became longer and the degree of difficulty exaggerated. But it was the spark that lit the fire and just five weeks later New Zealand's first Alpine Ironman was taking place on End Peak in the Matukituki Valley, just along from Treble Cone ski field. Lining up at the start were 34 men and one women, mostly, as Judkins delights in pointing out, friends. And they stayed that way. One of several unique features about any Judkins event is that he is always at the end, waiting to greet every finisher.

By 1983 the event had shifted to Mt Hutt, closer to the big population centre of Christchurch. Now it was a real race that brought out the best — and sometimes most intriguing — in Kiwi innovation. Racers had to ascend the Mt Hutt skifield on foot carrying their skis and then descend the other side, towards the Rakaia River. There were short skis, long skis, cross-country skis and alpine bindings, cross-country bindings and even bicycle toe-clips that running shoes were slipped into. Skiing styles varied wildly, too, not surprising given the equipment. The 1984 winner slowed himself by sitting on a mustering stick for braking and pointing straight down to the end of the snow line.

Then came a scramble down the scree slopes but race rules, few though they were in those days, declared skis had to be carried. Sam McLeod chopped his skis in half one year and stuffed the remnants into his rucksack. There was only one problem, they were his brother's nearly new skis and they'd been borrowed without permission. Next year the rules had changed — the skis had to reach the end of the run in one piece.

Coming off the scree slopes, competitors then had to run a few kilometres over green fields to reach the Rakaia River. There were no rapids through the seven kilometre long Rakaia Gorge but plenty of boils, eddies and whirlpools to catch the inexpert or unwary.

Finally there was the 16km cycle into Methven, beginning with a brutal 200 vertical metre hill climb. If you were lucky, a nor'wester would blow you into town.

The elements were all there, different sports, wild country and a set course that allowed improvisation within it. Copy-cat competitions began springing up all over the country.

But it was Judkins himself who made the next major leap forward with the Speights Coast to Coast as it is now known. Suddenly multisport had hurtled from an event lasting a few hours to one spread over two days. The concept of multi-day, multi-sport, commercial competition had been reached. At first light on the first day, competitors lined up on the beach at Kumara with their backs to the often wild and tempestuous Tasman Sea, ran frantically to reach their bikes in order to be off in an early bunch (Judkins likes to keep rules to a minimum, especially unenforceable ones like drafting) up the West Coast's main road link with Christchurch. At the Otira foot bridge, some 60km up the road, bikes are discarded for the run, if that's the word, more like boulder hopping, some would say, up the Deception and down the Mingha River valleys to Klondyke Corner, just out of Arthur's Pass. For some the legs are really hurting after riding too quickly and for others the adrenalin is still pumping after the fear and exhilaration of riding fast in a large pack. The overnight sleep is welcome and with luck there'll be no nightmares about Day Two.

This begins with another early start for a 16km cycle to the Waimakariri River and a 60km paddle through the Gorge. That only leaves another cycle, of 70km, to the Pacific Ocean at Sumner Beach and a heartfelt welcome from the irreverent Judkins. Since 1987 The Longest Day has also been available, the same course completed in a single day, after you've proved yourself in the two day event.

Hunt has competed eight times in the Speights Coast to Coast with a number of top 10 finishes. Stamina, endurance and consistency were obvious hallmarks. These were built up during the '70s.

After two years at university, Hunt moved to Queenstown and from 1973 to 1980 competed in freestyle skiing events in the United States and back home in Queenstown. He also organised a series of freestyle skiing events, Boogie in the Bumps, and ran freestyle skiing camps in the South Island. The seminal steps into event management had been taken.

In 1977 he started rafting and the following year became New Zealand's first registered Kiwi river guide. For the next 10 years or so he spent his summers rafting and winters skiing, sometimes as a heli-ski guide. He also climbed a number of South Island peaks, including Mount Tasman, and skied off some of them. He began taking part in ski touring expeditions and planned and led an expedition that climbed Papua New Guinea's highest peak, Mt Wilhelm (4509m), and descended the Watut River by raft. Three years later he led a New Zealand expedition down the Colorado River in the US and that same year, 1988, was a member of the New Zealand rafting team to the World Rafting Championships in Siberia.

His rafting skills and water safety credentials were well established. The following year, 1989, an unknown Frenchman with a wild dream arrived in New Zealand. He needed water safety skills like Hunt's. Adventure racing was about to become a worldwide reality.

The Frenchman was Gerard Fusil, a journalist and adventurer who had spent several years as media liaison on the annual Paris-Dakar car race. While on assignment in Patagonia, he had had a vision, a vision of teams of people moving through exotic, beautiful places under their own power. It would be easy to arrange, being in just one country, compared with the political and logistical problems of the Paris-Dakar moving through a number of different African countries. He had the germ of the idea, but where to put it into practice?

Fast forward to Perth and the America's Cup. Fusil was there, covering the French entry. He had plenty of time to think, to ponder and reflect, and he also had time to meet the Kiwi team. They told him about New Zealand, about the Coast to Coast and about the Kiwi love of the outdoors. They persuaded him to go to New Zealand and gave him a contact, Dave Bamford at Tourism Resource Consultants.

A former park ranger, Bamford had left with a colleague to form his own company. He had hiked, climbed and skied throughout the country and knew talented people everywhere. He was the ideal contact for Fusil.

Mind you, he was puzzled at first. A cryptic fax from Fusil talked about a 10 day rally in New Zealand, leading Bamford to think in terms of a car rally, not really part of his company philosophy which leaned more to the human friendly side of environmental use. But something caused him to pause and, intrigued and almost reluctantly, he agreed to a meeting.

He soon learned the truth — teams of five, human power, wild locations, adventure and challenge — and took the event seriously. The end result, in 1989, was the Grand Traverse, soon to become the Raid Gauloises, which ran from Lake Ohau to Manapouri, with many a detour along the way. The Water Safety Officer for the event was that Queenstown rafting guide, Geoff Hunt.

As Kiwi teams, thrown together quickly for the event, showed their mettle, blasting their mainly French adversaries into the proverbial weeds, Hunt watched closely and talked to the competitors before, during and after the race. And when it was all over, when the gloss and the glitter had faded, he talked some more and began asking a simple question: "Would you do this on an annual basis here in New Zealand?" And the answer was invariably "Yes." The concept had struck a chord.

Bamford looked at the concept, too, but uncertainty about the commercial viability, business commitments and the fact the race would need to be run far from his Wellington base saw him take a step back although he maintains a watchful, curious eye on the whole adventure racing scene (he was involved again later with Fusil, presenting him with the course for the Raid Gauloises in Sarawak).

Hunt had run small contests, managed a rafting company, organised rafting trips, all good training for organising an event that had the potential to be an international success. But the scale was bigger than he was used to, it was a big step up.

He worked, thought and planned and still it took two years. In 1991 the Southern Traverse was launched, following the trail of the Grand Traverse. The total distance was 312km and the winning team took just 40 hours and 57 minutes with only three hours sleep. Other teams straggled in over the next two days. But they loved it, loved the concept. For some, it is still the best race that's been but that is often the way with something new.

The race had a last minute course change the next year when a snow storm sitting on the Brodrick Pass forced a new start over the Haast Pass. Lake Ohau was the start again in 1993 but this time they left in the opposite direction, paddling down the lake — total distance 290km.

While the hard core had fallen in love with the event, it was still a battle to get the numbers. It was a steep learning curve and labour of love for racers, assistants and Geoff himself.

In 1994 the Traverse started and finished in Queenstown and a bad weather forecast forced a change to alternative routes and a shorter race at 232km. The next year saw an innovative start, from boats in the Milford Sound, and an abandoned final leg.Then the plan was to run up the Nevis Burn and cross into the South Wye but atrocious conditions with snow and bitter cold saw a racers' revolt and the last sections were abandoned.

In 1996 it was Te Anau's turn for the start with teams from the US and Japan lining up, too, eager to learn what was making the Kiwis seemingly invincible on the international adventure racing circuit. They finished as they started, in kayaks, across Lake Wakatipu to Queenstown — total distance 296km.

The next year, *el Niño* came to play, affecting the course dramatically. Starting at Makarora, racers trekked up two major alpine valleys — actually, one overseas team, on its first ever competition, never even made the first CP. They had a steep learning curve in front of them. Huge waves created by the ferocious winds forced a portage in the paddling section. Hurricane force winds and driving snow created overnight drama.

Then, in 1998, Geoff decided it was all too easy, the courses were too short. He wanted an event that would last at least four days and he succeeded for all but the winning team.

Some were complaining about the length, mostly in terms of the time needed, getting that week or more off work, especially support crews who don't get the same direct pleasure and benefit. But for Rob Nagle, "it was the perfect length, long enough to require mental strength but not so long as to be physically debilitating." He, despite winning the Raid in Ecuador, like many others found that race just too long, too physically demanding and debilitating.

But, assuming the Southern Traverse is now the 'right length' and last year's course was 'the best yet,' how does Geoff actually design his courses? How is he planning this year's route in Nelson?

"The course comes together section by section," he says, "but always with the end in mind."

It is not a matter of working backwards, more a matter of choosing a number of possible starting points and then following a course to the end. This is first done on maps, tracing routes that allow the various disciplines to link naturally. Normally he will try to have at least two sections of each discipline — mountain running, mountain biking and kayaking are the principles plus possibles like abseiling, rafting, caving and climbing on fixed ropes. Horses have been used here and in the Raid and EcoChallenge. And always there will be the route finding challenge. This seems to be the key to success now. As they say of orienteering, "It's better to walk in the right direction than to run the opposite way."

So he looks on the map, "We can start on bikes here," he thinks, "and ride to this river. Then we pull out here and trek over this mountain range. It looks steep and gnarly, some big cliffs, so I might be able to add an abseil here. And there are some deep caves over here. I wonder what the Department of Conservation will say to that?" And so it goes. Then he'll try a different start, or the same start but disciplines in a different order so the route is quite different. And finally, when he's happy on the map, it's time to try it on the ground.

And that's important. Every competitor can be sure that someone has been over the entire course and that someone is usually Geoff himself, checking routes, sorting Check Points and thinking always about safety.

"You have to differentiate between triathlons and adventure racing. For us, there's no ambulance on standby.

"It is important to maintain elements of danger, people want to be challenged. And be surprised." Just the same, it is incumbent on every team to be able to see to the first aid of any member in an emergency. Severe weather can turn the tamest course into a potential death trap.

But who does he design the course for? "Myself," is the simple answer. And that is why the Traverse has earned its reputation as a competitors' course, Geoff is the only international adventure race designer who can claim a second placing in the Raid and a fourth in the EcoChallenge. Impressive results that put him in the top echelon of international adventure racers.

Navigation is crucial

"Navigation is crucial," said Race Director Geoff Hunt. The warning went out in the pre-race newsletters and received renewed emphasis at the last briefing. And he wasn't joking.

The team that had the sharpest navigation in the 1998 Southern Traverse was Long International, of Queenstown, covering the 418km of kayaking, caving, mountain biking and mountain walking in $91^1/_2$ hours, six and a half hours clear of the next team.

"We were just three mates out for a four day adventure in the hills," said team member Hadyn Key. The other mates were Aiden Craig and Tim Grammer, all friends from their earlier, surf lifesaving days in Mt Maunganui. In truly democratic fashion, there was no team leader. They were very much a team of equals. "The focus was enjoyment, not winning. We wanted to have a good time." They had a good time — and still they left foot prints for the others to follow.

Steve Gurney was particularly delighted to see them at the finish. "We kept following these foot prints," he said. "We were afraid they might have belonged to phantoms."

A record number of 42 teams from eight countries lined up in perfect conditions on the beach at Lake Manapouri, distant mountains reflected in the water. Only the bravest, observers or competitors, were prepared to pick a winner. This was the strongest line up yet. Cromwell were back to defend their title. Wet Coast dropped out because of equipment failure with the finish line almost in view the year before — after leading the whole way. They had a score to settle. Formthotics consisted of Steve Gurney, Ian Adamson and Rob Nagle. With John Howard and Robin Benincasa they'd just won the toughest Raid Gauloises ever in Ecuador and competed in a multi-day stage race in China. This was the top adventure racing team in the world but they were also tired, physically and mentally. And there were always the dark horses.

These days, many people have the required physical skills for adventure racing. Longer races like the Southern Traverse, however, require ever tougher mental skills, the ability to choose the best route and know when to sleep and when to go, these decisions being made quickly at times of severe stress and massive sleep deprivation. These are not ideal times for lucid judgement. That left the question, who was best prepared mentally for the challenges ahead?

Even at the start, there was a question — would there be enough water in the river? Days of unusually fine, rainless weather had lowered lake and river levels but "there was a jet boat up the Waiau yesterday," said Hunt, "there won't be a problem." And mostly there wasn't, apart from the one or two who took a bad line and discovered some metal stakes in the river that ripped open their expensive kevlar boats, a bit like peeling an orange. Or a banana. Duct tape can only do so much.

Others found different problems, like overhanging willows and unexpected eddies. Even three times and defending champion Bill Godsall of Team Cromwell suffered the ignominious overturn when the front of his boat caught an eddy and the back was swept over by the current. Harald Zundel, a US Navy graduate taking a year off to travel the world adventure racing, earned himself the unfortunate sobriquet of 'U-boat Captain' because of the number of times he inspected the river bottom. By the time he got to the rapids below the Monowai suspension bridge, his lips were blue and he was shivering with cold. Food, fluid and a jacket saw him quickly back on the river and when he finally arrived at the transition at Clifden he was warm again and happy — and there were still 11 teams behind him.

One team was so far behind, in fact, it had to be rescued. East Dream, a Japanese women's team, was back to avenge a defeat two years earlier. They had the skills but not the strength nor attitude. Nonchalantly cruising down the Waiau River they were eventually pulled off after dark by safety boats.

Second off the river, Long International were fastest through transition and on to the bikes, starting with a kind of scenic detour, New Zealand's first adventure racing cave experience, a stroll through the limestone wonders of the Waiau Caves. For most it was a pleasant interlude but one woman, who also capsized in the river, needed to be wedged between her team mates.

The first mountain bike section encompassed fields, farm roads and forestry tracks. Some 67km long, it also entailed some tricky navigation through the Rowallan Forest. It was even trickier than expected, it turned out, much to the chagrin of, for example, the vastly experienced John Knight. Teamed this year with two Brazilian women, he was seen at one stage with a bike on each shoulder, bashing through bush in the middle of the night — and then not seen again for some time. He took nearly 20 hours for a section his former team mate Hadyn Key did in just over five hours. But most competitors admitted to a minimum of half an hour lost through bad navigation.

The next transition was in the Lillburn Valley, on the way to Lake Hauroko. While Knight and many others were spending the night bush bashing, Long International and the other lead teams were pushing on, stopping only long enough to refuel and change. Ahead of them was a section of challenging navigation that required real skill in compass work and map reading. It started through a plantation and then the route disappeared under the dense canopy of the Dean Forest. There was little variation underfoot, a few streams but no hills to orientate from. As usual, the front teams had little difficulty.

"There wasn't even much of a problem with windblown trees," said Team Cromwell's Jim Cotter. "They can be tiring." And put you very slightly off course if you're not careful. Missing a CP in dense bush by 100 metres is just as bad as missing it by a kilometre.

Slower, less experienced teams, never even made it to the CP, eventually returning to the Lillburn Valley.

"I practise learning exactly where I am on the map," said Key later. "If you don't know where you are, how can you find a Check Point?" Obviously, many of the teams didn't know where they were and admitted later they needed to do a lot more to improve their navigation skills. Especially at night.

From Blue Hankie Corner, as the CP was whimsically called, the route led deeper into Fiordland, climbing to the top of Hindley Peak, overlooking Lake Monowai. Navigation got easier, with ridges to climb and follow and the early teams had the benefit of daylight, although the cloud base was low - and getting lower. Formthotics was the only early team to rest at the transition, snatching an hour's sleep on the wool bales in the wool shed. They left two hours behind Long International but had caught up by the abseil on the north side of Hindley Peak — that was the sleep of experience.

The abseil consisted of two sections, one 100 metres and the other 85 metres, with spectacular views over Lake Monowai although the high peaks were obscured by the lowering cloud. Most teams finished the abseil — which some teams found a bit dodgy with loose rocks — and descended to the lakeshore before slogging round the side to the next transition at the lake outlet. This section was to see a few accidents, too. Like Ian Binney, from Team Five and Bit, slipping down a small bluff and breaking a wrist (fortunately there was a doctor in the team) and Dan O'Shea, ex-Navy Seal and team mate of the U-boat Captain, collecting a rock on his shoulder that put him out.

"We tried 50 to 100 metres above the lake shore in the hope of finding easier going but it was hopeless," said Key. "In the end we came back to the shore and spent half the time wading through the mud and water," like water buffalo knee deep in a rice padi pulling the plough. Long International were still first out to the Transition Area.

High drama was being played out behind the three leaders. The consistent and popular Macpac team, of Christchurch, another 5-person group, had been making their usual good time, keeping the other teams honest. Then Andy MacBeth started having breathing difficulties and his asthma inhaler wasn't helping. He'd had problems in the EcoChallenge in Morocco and obviously hadn't fully recovered. His team mates were worried by the top of the abseil, anxious for medical advice. They pushed on to the Transition Area with MacBeth's chest infection worsening and he almost collapsed twice on that last brutal walk. And then they pulled out — a difficult decision for these strong competitors. But they didn't leave the race, they love it too much for that. Team members kept popping up at various Transition Areas to offer encouragement and advice.

This year there was another Macpac team, a unique outfit — Macpac Geographic. This team had a special mission. It was the focus for a documentary on the race for National Geographic's Explorer Channel which can be accessed by hundreds of millions of viewers worldwide. Channel presenter Boyd Matson, 51-years-old, had done a number of extreme running adventures for the cameras, including the five day Sahara ultra-marathon. This time he was teamed up with a bunch of Dunedin-based Traverse veterans, veterans in both age and experience.

"I thought I was in a good team," said Matson. "They told me they start slow and taper off. That's not true." Indeed not, those guys are competitors to the finish.

His pre-race training was hardly ideal, running on roads and riding a stationary bike but he felt fit and was looking forward to the challenge. He knew at least he was in capable hands. But he began to wonder about the event, the people who take part in it and himself on the first night when a wrong turn in the Rowallan Forest began a mini-epic of bush bashing that brought them back to the start of the bash — two hours later.

"I really began to understand the race on the second night, in the rain, trying to get up Hindley Peak," he said. "I didn't expect it to be so hard pushing through the bush. It's not open like the North California forests I'm used to. It's very hard on the feet and the legs."

Too hard.

An exhausted Matson reluctantly pulled the plug and returned to the Lillburn Transition, admitting defeat with a profound respect for the other competitors. And how did his new-found team mates feel? "Like shit. The worst we have ever felt. Not finishing ruined our record [as Arrow International]. It was the best ever course and we desperately wanted to do the entire race."

That left part of the National Geographic film crew stranded on Hindley Peak — literally. Dropped there by the legendary local helicopter pilot Bill Black, they were sitting in thick cloud. And so were Black and his chopper — for two days until the mist rose enough to allow safe flight.

HiTec Canterbury also pulled out on this leg — but this is a tale with a funny ending. The team found Blue Hankie corner without difficulty and pushed on to be in the last of the bush near the top of Hindley Peak in the rain with night falling. It was time to check the map. The map? The map was lost. Under the now severe conditions, retreat was felt to be the sensible course. The three of them turned around and headed back down the stream. Strangely, it began to feel different, the bush was thicker and harder to get through, the terrain steeper but they were committed now, they had no choice. Wherever the stream went, it would eventually lead them out.

Sunrise, Lake Te Anau

*Wye Creek
with the finish in
the distance*

Inflatable canoes, Raid Gauloises, Sarawak

On horseback, Raid Gauloises, Patagonia

Murray Thomas, Southern Traverse

Clearwater Cave, Raid Gauloises, Sarawak

Left: Grebe Valley, Fiordland

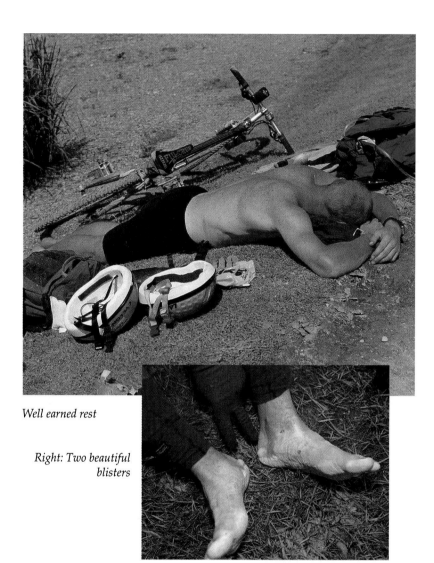

Well earned rest

*Right: Two beautiful
blisters*

With daylight they found themselves on a farm track but nothing looked familiar which was not surprising since they'd crossed into the Dean Burn watershed instead of following the Hindley back down. And then, as they approached a farm, an apparition appeared, the Reverend Jocelyn Bron bearing hot tea and Girl Guide biscuits. And the news they'd almost walked back to Clifden. Oh, the embarrassment!

The front teams weren't having much fun either. Long International and Formthotics stayed in Monowai just long enough to eat and change before heading out on their mountain bikes, determined to make as much of the route round the southern flanks of the rugged, starkly beautiful Takitimu Mountains in daylight. Wet Coast opted for an hour's sleep and left hard on Formthotics' rear wheels, the latter having made another of their lightning transitions.

But they hadn't gone far before a bitter southerly front came through, dropping temperatures with chilling rain that also caused the mountain streams to rise rapidly. And it turned the forestry and farm tracks into mud so that more than half the route to the next transition at Aparima Forks was pushing or carrying. It's no wonder, then, that this section was almost universally disliked. Even the top teams found it hard going but one of the race's high points was also included. You can imagine the joy, after battling the elements through the night, of arriving at the Rock Hut CP to find a roaring fire and cups of hot tea and coffee, courtesy of the race officials there.

You might also spare a thought for a number of other teams, huddled under flimsy tent-fly shelters, trying to find a reprieve from the driving wind and rain. With fiendish cunning, the elements unerringly found the smallest chinks to torment the already frustrated racers. They were forced to wait until daylight to safely cross tiny streams that had turned into raging, roiling torrents, the sound of rocks and boulders carried along by the current clearly audible. It was a potential death trap under those conditions of night and storm.

By the time the three leaders rolled into Aparima on a grey and misty Wednesday morning, there were teams spread behind them all the way back to Lillburn transition and Race Director Geoff Hunt was having to dust off his contingency plans. Statistically, one third of competitors finish the whole course, one third complete a shortened course and one third are unranked (they lose a member or two) or fail to finish. This year would prove the same.

Exhausted from their nocturnal exertions, the three lead teams all gave themselves up to brief sleeps before setting out again , this time on foot. Ahead was an ascent of the northern end of the Takitimus, round the shoulders of Clare Peak and down to Princhester Hut. It wasn't far, just 22km which Hunt reckoned would take seven hours on average. But it was to become an epic.

The mist was thick as Long International, Wet Coast and Formthotics left Aparima, the mountains completely obscured. Time limped soddenly and the next batch of teams began to filter in slowly, cold and hungry. Mountain streams go down after the rain as quickly as they rise with it. As first light came, the swollen torrent became fordable and the teams that had huddled under their flimsy shelters unbent themselves, shook out kinks, stretched aching muscles and pushed on. Later teams were more fortunate, not having to wait at all. Even so, competitors continued to dislike the section, the pushing, scrambling and carrying.

Gear was wet and uncomfortable. A J Hacket's support crew spread the team's tent fly over the open bonnet of a vehicle, motor running, in an attempt to dry it before the next mountain run. Actually, that support crew had fun with vehicles. Later that day they filled up with petrol on the way to the next transition. The only problem was, they had a diesel. Or was it the other way round? Whatever, the two fuels don't mix and fuel tank cleaning was suddenly essential. And then the gas station's machine refused their credit card. Who said the racers have all the excitement?

Up on the Takitimus, visibility had, if that were possible, got worse as the three lead teams looked unsuccessfully for CP16 below Clare Peak. In increasingly bitter conditions, they individually retraced their steps and checked out all possibilities before eventually giving up and struggling on. It was still hazardous, however, as Wet Coast later reported: "There were a lot of dangerous bluffs, very difficult to make out in the conditions. We had problems finding a safe exit off the tops."

And then, contrary to expectations, they dropped straight down into the West Princhester Creek and walked round the fields to approach the Transition Area from the north. "It was too difficult under the conditions to traverse round and try and hit the Bog Burn track."

Back up in the dense fog and wind, there were now several teams casting round, checking bearings and looking for the Check Point. Four teams, including Cromwell and HiTec Geraldine, actually got together and set up a grid search where they expected the CP to be. Nothing. Hours went by, bodies grew cold and food and fluid were in short supply. Hypothermia was becoming a distinct possibility for the under-equipped and the undernourished. It is amazing how many athletes interpret a minimum gear requirement as a maximum, they won't take more.

"I always pack spare polyprops for an emergency like that," Bill Godsall said later. "They weigh nothing and might save a life." Certainly someone had reason to be thankful Bill was carrying the extra gear that awful night.

Down at the Princhester TA, support crew were becoming increasingly agitated. "Where are they?" "Why are they taking so long?" Nobody knew and there was no answer from the Check Point. Wednesday night passed and finally more teams emerged from off the hill, telling tales of misery and frustration. Doyles Outdoors was the last team to come in, change and head out on the bikes and thus be on schedule to complete the entire course. Later teams had missed the cut-off.

Long International took nearly 10 hours for that seven hour section. Others were out in the murk for over 20 hours.

It was sunny off the mountain in the Transition Area, a marked contrast to what was happening on the tops, when Graham Tanner arrived. Except he was supposed to be manning the missing CP. In the thick fog, and despite his considerable experience manning CPs on the Southern Traverse and as part of a mountain rescue team, he had been unable to find the right site so the competitors had been searching for a phantom, non-existent CP. He was, not surprisingly, feeling 'absolutely gutted' and extremely embarrassed.

One team lodged a protest about the missing CP and the hours spent searching for it. But as Murray Thomas, of Team Valet Services, which probably devoted more time than any other to the search, including dropping below the bush line to sleep briefly in more benign surroundings, said: "Everybody suffered, not just one team, even if teams spent different amounts of time looking. That's adventure racing. Accept it and move on."

There's one thing you can be sure of, though. Race Director Hunt won't allow a problem like that again. Many solutions have been mooted and they all seem to include GPS, helicopters and a marker of some kind.

Long International completed the ride to 9-mile Bay on Lake Te Anau comfortably in the lead and proceeded to put in what was to be the fastest paddle up the lake, in windless, moonlit conditions, to Te Anau Downs. There they finally stopped, put their heads down "for a long sleep" — of an hour and a half or so — before setting out on the last, long walk at first light. Wet Coast and Formthotics were several hours behind them and the sun was well and truly up by the time they began their paddle, still in almost glassy conditions.

Sleep deprivation does strange things sometimes, creates strange appetites — and also allows support crews to show their dedication and devotion. At 8:30 on a gloriously sunny Thursday morning, Wet Coast members variously stuffed down hot chips brought up from Te Anau, a meat pie and apricots on toast. Then, in a psychological ploy, they set out quickly, walked a couple of kilometres and crashed in the bushes for a sleep. Nobody's quite sure who they fooled. Or if they were comfortable.

The walk from Te Anau Downs to Mavora Lakes turned out to be the highlight for many of the competitors. Hunt designed it to be a navigational challenge with two mountain ranges to cross. The direct route over the Dunton Range was particularly difficult. Most of the teams recognised this and outsmarted Hunt, opting instead for the longer, flatter route around the south end of the Duntons and up the Upukerora River. Although it was perhaps 15km longer it was much easier with no route finding problems. Instead, competitors waxed lyrical about the birds, the deer and the fish in the river pools.

With a CP at Acheron Lakes (which Long International interpreted slightly differently, going instead to a point listed with different co-ordinates and, not surprisingly, not finding anyone there. After the Takitimu disaster, they weren't going to waste time looking too hard.) the Livingston Mountains had to be crossed — with, for the luckiest ones — a full moon.

"It was so bright," said Wet Coast, "we could read the map by it. We could even distinguish the colours."

Long International got up on top in daylight. "There was a spectacular sunset and moonrise," said Key. "We could see Te Anau and Fiordland to the west, the Takitimus to the south and Mavora Lakes before us. I'd love to go back there camping."

But there was a penalty to pay. After a minimum of 15 hours of walking, feet were swollen, sore and blistered. The last thing they wanted to do was go downhill — especially steeply. But there was a descent of around 1000 vertical metres down steep, tussock faces. Feet screamed with agony. That was followed by a trudge of several kilometres on a soft, gravel track, beside the beckoning waters of North Mavora Lake, to the last Transition Area (and fresh coffee provided free by a Queenstown café — bliss!).

Hadyn Key hallucinated down this stretch. "I'd been there before [two years earlier the Traverse went the opposite way on MTBs] and knew there were no turn-offs. For the first time in the race, there was no need to concentrate. My mind switched off totally and I hallucinated. It wasn't a problem, I knew the track would end at the Transition."

And so it did. When Long International arrived at the last transition just before 1:30 on Thursday morning the trio were totally exhausted, eyes unfocused, unable to concentrate. Their support crew lovingly surrounded them, drove away the gawking crowd of racers, support crew and media who were still awake, fed them, nursed them and eased aching, swollen feet into bike shoes that were now a size or two too small. Just 55 minutes later they wobbled off into the stygian black, three narrow beams casting minimal light in front of them.

Only 3hrs 10mins later, with the first glimmerings of dawn fingering the sky, Hadyn Key, Aiden Craig and Tim Grammer crossed the finish line at Walter Peak, 91hrs 30mins and at least 418 km after setting out from Fraser's Beach on Lake Manapouri. The next teams hadn't even finished their mountain walk.

Wet Coast was next into Mavora Lakes, arriving around 06:30. Like Long International, they looked exhausted and changing into bike gear was a struggle. Nevertheless, they rode out confident at least of second place overall. Certainly there were no challengers for the first 5-person team home.

A little more than an hour later, as the valley fog was beginning to lift, Formthotics strolled into camp looking fit and fresh. They'd had an hour or two's sleep on the trek and it showed. In 26 minutes they'd fed, drunk a coffee and changed and were off, chasing Wet Coast.

Formthotics had not gone far when they spied bodies lying on the side of the road. Unbelievably, it was Wet Coast. Rather than risk serious injury falling asleep and crashing, they'd stopped their bikes and were sleeping. Utter fatigue had finally caught up with them and overall second place was lost, that confidence had been misplaced.

Throughout the day and following night until 10:00 on Saturday morning, exactly five days after the start, teams kept arriving. Fourteen had completed the entire course, the rest one of several shortened versions, a system designed to allow all teams to cross the finish line. The last team to cross the line having completed the whole course was Team Outward Bound, exhausted, elated and bubbling with enthusiasm about the last trek. They'll be back.

The tourists gathering at Walter Peak on Friday afternoon must have been puzzled. Under that bright, early summer sun, brightly, tightly, lycra-clad groups of three or five were riding their bicycles into the frigid waters of Lake Wakatipu. Others, often stripped to the waist with white, wrinkled, blistered feet bared to dry, were cast upon the manicured lawns, finally getting the sleep their exhausted bodies had been craving for days.

In their own words

Whatever the event, competitors always have a multiplicity of reasons for being there, probably as many reasons as there are entrants. The same goes for their expectations, whether of themselves, their team or the event itself.

For many racers, being in the Southern Traverse is a natural progression. Talk to competitors before the event and the ideas of challenge, adventure and a good time come to the fore. Others want "to test personal limits." Overseas athletes speak of the race's international reputation and there's nothing better nor more honest than word of mouth recommendation. Other reasons for competing include:

▼ We needed something to do.

▼ A mate talked me into it and then pulled out.

▼ A distorted sense of reality.

▼ The lawns needed mowing.

▼ Mid-life crisis.

▼ Any excuse for a week off work.

▼ Seemed a good idea in June.

▼ This could be the first and last. It has been such a huge commitment of time and money that I'm not sure I could justify it again.

▼ To finish the goddamned event in one piece and to brag to one and all how good it was. One tends to remember only The Good Bits.

▼ Saves Government funds caring for the mentally impaired now there's no money for hospital beds.

For one Japanese woman it is "a kind of revenge after failing two years ago. I want to discover myself, push my limits and spread out my world."

And finally, "this kind of race is an excellent life experience that leads you to get along better with your party, admire nature, get to know yourself better and have fun."

Expectations of personal achievements usually revolve around overcoming mental and physical exhaustion and "to see how far I can be pushed." "And survive" seems to be understood. One person, however, is "so knackered from preparation that tiredness is not a new thing" but does confess that "sleep deprivation could be interesting." Everyone wants to "work as a team and have fun."

Expectations about the course itself show more variations:

▼ That the course is kept secret ... is beautiful, challenging and with a few little surprises added.

▼ There will be long and difficult navigation in terrible weather.

▼ It will be tough, longer than we think.

▼ We will travel through magnificent country in gruelling conditions.

▼ It will be hard but hopefully achievable.

▼ Remote, scary and beautiful.

▼ Very tough, very long, a bit like staring down the dangerous end of a loaded, double-barrel shotgun.

A few racers admit to binge training, by which, presumably, they mean late, isolated and intense bursts of activity. Most have been more sensible, putting in long hours and big distances, "long, slow, steady stuff" as one puts it. Overnight training has been popular as well as time together as a team when possible. Few mention specific training and even fewer talk of night navigation practice. Given the problems some will have with navigation in daylight, let alone the nocturnal variety, perhaps they'll get that practice next time?

But all this is before the race, part of the preparation and the mental baggage some carry into the event. How well will expectations succeed against harsh reality? How many dreams will be rudely shattered and how many will do better than they expect?

As the teams finally cross the finish line, the principal feeling is one of elation, sometimes coupled with relief "to have finished with five people intact." As the initial euphoria wears off, a few practicalities intrude, from "we've all got sore feet" to a laconic, understated, "the body's taken a few knocks."

Many competitors agree "the first two or three days were the worst but it got better" and they were, as expected, "pushed by sleep deprivation." Puzzled, one competitor asks, "How do you train for an event like this?" The answer, someone else explains, is that "you have to do one first to know what to train for." Perhaps they'll both do better next time.

For one first timer, "this has been the biggest physical challenge I've ever undertaken and the greatest sporting triumph." A race veteran says simply: "Good hard fun. Every time I do one of these I forget how long and hard they are." Another is a little disappointed: "it wasn't quite as epic and in the backblocks as previous years." This is a lone voice, however, more people being inclined to the view that this course was "the best ever, a benchmark difficult to exceed." And "the Southern Traverse is now world class. It ranks as the toughest event on the world circuit and it has retained its special attribute as a race designed for competitors." Which can make it difficult for neophytes: "It was a much tougher race than I imagined with very technical navigation." Well, yes, but the pre-race literature was full of warnings of the need for navigation skills. Most people accepted this but still didn't do enough preparation and will work on navigation for next time. A solitary voice, who shall remain anonymous, calls for harder navigation.

How will competitors prepare in the future? Most are reasonably happy with the work they'd done, apart from the need to be better at navigating, especially at night. Then come calls for more team training and more off-track tramping, both in the bush and in the mountains. Long weekend tramps will include sleep deprivation experience by keeping moving right through the night. Tongue in cheek, or should that be foot in shoe, someone suggests he (or she) will "trek longer in wet shoes while eating less for training." Perhaps they are just being realistic.

Then there are calls for:

▼ More sleep before the event.

▼ More support crew.

▼ No hired equipment.

▼ More paddling down rivers in tippy boats.

A worthwhile (but perhaps not always practical) suggestion for Geoff Hunt, indeed all race organisers, rather than competitors is that "bike legs should be either fast and fun (to get somewhere) or technical and rideable or very scenic."

Because the event seems to have such a high overall happiness rating, it is difficult for competitors to select individual moments of great joy. There are some, however, and they include:

▼ Biking in the moonlight.

▼ Moonsets.

▼ Moonrises.

▼ Seeing the sun rise over the misty valleys of the Takitimus.

▼ The Acheron Lakes.

▼ Arriving at Transition Areas because of the encouraging crew.

▼ Arriving into ANY Transition Area.

▼ The roaring fire and hot drinks at Rock Hut.

Bad memories tend to fade quickly but, while still fresh in their minds, racers recall:

▼ Not finishing, it ruined our record.

▼ Pulling out.

▼ Sitting under a tent fly at night with a creek flowing under us.

▼ The wife won't let me do it again.

▼ Bush bashing for 13 hours from the abseil to the Lake Monowai Transition Area.

▼ Navigating at night.

▼ The flat walk on gravel beside a lake you could paddle on.

▼ Slow transitions.

▼ Paddling a Puffin.

▼ Pushing my bike up endless, continuous, muddy, steep, relentless hills.

The last word, however, goes to the first time competitor, hit fair between the eyes by a reality the veterans know all too well: "I thought it would be a once in a lifetime opportunity but now I realise I am hooked." He — or she — is still able to be realistic and practical, however. "But I must book myself in for a navigation course."

Unsung heroes

"I have a profound new respect for support crews," says Kathy Sassin, world class adventure racer and neophyte support crew member. After narrowly being beaten into second place in the 1998 Raid Gauloises by a team containing two Kiwis, John Howard and Steve Gurney, Kathy came to New Zealand for the Southern Traverse — but as support crew.

"I understand better now," she says, "why support crew don't always have exactly the right piece of equipment, type of food, replacement drink or whatever I want, immediately when I want it, if not sooner. Support crews have their own problems, they work hard and lose sleep, too."

"Should every competitor spend time on a support crew?"

Kathy laughs. "Maybe they should."

Top local racer and Southern Traverse veteran Adam Fairmaid, out this year through injury, is also along this year like Kathy in the unfamiliar role of support crew. He echoes her sentiments and adds, "I've put on 3 kilos because I've not been competing or exercising."

Support crew, along with race assistants, are the unsung heroes and heroines of adventure racing. Few racers realise quite how much they owe their personal success to their crew. Nor that they suffer the same emotional highs and lows they go through themselves.

Before the '98 Traverse, one North Island support crew listed their expectations quite succinctly:

▼ That they (the team) don't have any injuries and achieve their goals, both personal and as a team.

▼ That we perform beyond the race team's expectations, do a bloody good job.

▼ That I will remain calm and work efficiently toward providing all the necessary support to our 5-person team.

▼ We haven't travelled this far and spent this much money without blood and sweat and tears.

One veteran support crew member was especially voluble and effusive talking about crews in general and his own role in particular.

"Any book on adventure racing," he says, "needs five chapters on assistants."

Exactly as racers compete "just once to realise a personal goal" and then realise they're hooked, so, too, do many assistants discover an addictive element in helping competitors. "There is the satisfaction of helping, of anticipating requests, passing on something before it is actually asked for."

Support crew also run through the whole gamut of emotions, just like their race team. They get high, feel happy when their team makes up time but then depression can set in as they wait. Where is their team? They should have been here an hour ago. There are strong winds on the tops, maybe a severe storm raging up there. Have the team found shelter? Has there been an accident or is there some other kind of problem? Tired and anxious, pressures mounting, the various support crews then begin to help each other, supporting support crews. And then the relief when the team finally arrives, intact, out of the mist or the bush or wherever.

Because the event lasts several days, sleep deprivation can also play a part, and make driving from one transition to the next a hazard, a good argument for restricting driving times for support crews, and, just like the competitors, their emotions swing up and down.

When the team is in the Transition Area, jobs are clear cut. It's after the teams have left the logistical problems begin all over again. There may be food to buy — necessitating a lengthy detour, perhaps — repairs to be made to equipment and washing and drying of clothing.

And, just as for the racers, there is the problem of getting the time off work. With the Traverse now a good day longer than before, many of the assistants are beginning to ask if the event isn't too long, if they can justify the time spent off work.

One of the most popular descriptions for competitors talking about the Traverse is 'camaraderie,' the sharing of experiences with like minded individuals, 'mutual trust and sociability of comrades,' according to the Concise Oxford Dictionary. The same is true of support crews, especially, perhaps, the 'sociability' aspect. This is often necessary as anxious assistants fret and worry, wondering where their teams are. Many of these crews have come back year after year and they, too, enjoy the chance to catch up on the past year, chat, gossip, if you will, and share the excitement of being integral members of a team.

Support crews are thus getting friendlier to each other, closer together. They share gear and experiences and support each other when teams don't arrive, the weather is foul or the race organisation can't give them exactly the answer they want to hear.

That's the fun side, the social side, if you like, but how does it all come together, how does it work? It is worth noting that many teams, often those that have not performed to expectations, have regretted not including their support crews earlier.

'Spud' Godsall, Bill's wife — her name is Irene but nobody seems to know it — missed the first Traverse but has been along for every one since "and I still enjoy it or I wouldn't keep coming back." Actually, it's a family affair with daughter Kelly now having taken over the baking of the fruitcake (life support for hungry writers and photographers as well as racers). Their system has been honed, if not to perfection at least to something like it, a method that has proved itself over time.

The first thing you notice at the Godsall camp is the sheer number of people, they're there to support each other as well as the team and to have a great time doing it.

"We have a meeting two weeks before the event," says Spud. "There we sort out our roles. We have two [assistants] for each athlete and then there are two floaters, two people who can fetch and carry, run errands, whatever else is suddenly needed.

"And at that time the spare bedroom becomes Race HQ. The bikes and all the gear are put in and sorted. Then, just before we leave, I go on a big shopping expedition for the whole team." These days the Cromwell team includes members from Queenstown and Australia but Spud has learned their likes and dislikes. This is extremely important because the athletes have to be able to enjoy their food and each has his own idiosyncrasies. They need vast quantities because of their energy demands but its all too easy when you're stressed and exhausted to forgo food if it's unappetising — and compound the problems.

When the support crew arrive at the next Transition Area, perhaps having had to detour for many kilometres to fetch a spare part, a new tyre, a special food request or wash and dry race clothing, they have to put up camp, rain, hail or shine. The gear and clothing for the next section have to be readied.

Estimated times are given for all sections. Sometimes racers are unbelievably fast, far ahead of schedule, and they'll arrive tired, hungry and expecting food and everything ready. Or it's taken much longer because they couldn't find a CP, the rivers were up and the route was much harder to find anyway — and they still come in tired, (extra) hungry and expecting food. It's a no win situation, in some ways.

"We always try and have hot food waiting," says Spud. "Especially in cold conditions. But you have to be — and we always are — ready and able to change on request." You also need the medications, the ointments, creams and plasters that need to be applied.

And when the racers have eaten, maybe had a quick nap, changed into their gear for the next section and headed out again, the tent has to come down again, camp needs cleaning up and the whole circus hits the road to the next Transition Area.

Long International's support crew, all first timers but obviously well coached, can have the final word. "It was loads of fun, tiring and awesome, all at once. Next year we're going to get a campervan."

Personal reflections

Hadyn Key — list maker

"You can learn a lot from every race," says Hadyn Key, "if you realise what's actually happening. You can take that on board or you can leave it. I like to take as much on board as I can."

And in his brief acquaintance with multisport and adventure racing he has shown just how true that is. His attitude approaches the cerebral, he thinks all the time when competing, "Where am I? Where do we go next? When should we sleep?" Despite that, he always wants to enjoy himself, both in competition — "Four days in the hills with a couple of mates" is how he describes the 1998 Southern Traverse — and training. These days he's trying to train smarter and more specifically. You need to think carefully what you really need to achieve, he says, and "do what you enjoy and have fun."

Having fun is crucial for Hadyn. He's no hedonist but he has a wonderful zest for life that bubbles forth whenever you talk to him. The question is, how has he channelled this vivacity into the adventure racing machine that won the 1998 Southern Traverse so clearly?

Like most Gisborne boys, he was right into surfing and, at the age of 14, started lifesaving. To be successful he was swimming regularly in the pool, getting up early before school to put in the kilometres, and in the winter he was flat water paddling. He was learning discipline and building a base fitness. He represented New Zealand in surf life saving in 1987 and paddled as a junior.

At the age of 20, he discovered skiing. He spent the winter of 1992 in Wanaka and then, in 1993, shifted to Queenstown where he still lives.

Life was good with like-minded friends and myriad adventures on the doorstep. Nevertheless, with his disciplined background, he started looking for something else, a new endeavour, and found it in the Kepler Challenge, a 67 kilometres mountain run at Te Anau. Despite never having done even a marathon run before he enjoyed himself and the following year, 1995, began training for the event again. Unknowingly, he had taken his first step on to the adventure racing path.

Then, just four weeks before that year's Southern Traverse, he was asked by resident Frenchman Eric Billoud to join his Ooh La La team. Hadyn quickly added cycling and paddling to his training schedule and, while Aiden Craig was away, quietly borrowed his bike because it was lighter. The team led into the Nevis Valley and up towards the South Wye before the race was halted because of the atrocious conditions of snow and ice. Ooh La La was awarded first place.

Hadyn was hooked. First place in his first adventure race and he was just having fun. A few weeks later he ran the Kepler Challenge again.

From Christchurch, that bright, shining beacon the Coast to Coast was making its siren call. Following his Traverse and Kepler successes, he was granted dispensation by Robin Judkins and went straight into the Longest Day, the one day event, coming home a very creditable 19th. Less tactical and mentally demanding than the Traverse, it is, comparatively, a sprint and it was "a huge learning experience." More entries went on to Hadyn's mental lists. He is a compulsive list maker, part of the key to his success.

For the 1996 Southern Traverse he teamed up with another couple of locals, sports shop owner — and formerly New Zealand's premier Ironman — John Knight and optometrist Adam Fairmaid. "We began training months out from the event, starting with one hour bike rides together up to 15 hour combined bike/runs or bush work."

But they were pipped at the post by three minutes by the world's top adventure racing team, Eco-Internet/Fairydown, despite having made up a huge amount of time by going over Walter Peak instead of round on the penultimate section. On reflection, however, "we pushed too hard early on, we pushed beyond our limits. We moved at a pace that felt good but a video replay would reveal appalling mistakes and constant stops. You have to realise where that point is and we're starting to work that out now. We should have stopped earlier and had a sleep, we would have made up that sleep time in a couple of hours."

Aggrieved by their narrow loss the previous year, Outdoor Sport were out to make amends in the 1997 Traverse. The weather had other ideas, thanks to *el Niño* . Along with the other lead teams they were battered unmercifully by hurricane force winds on the Pisa Range and then, when they finally did emerge, Adam was forced to withdraw with hernias. Hadyn and John kept going with their friends in Cromwell (Bill Godsall, Jim Cotter and Eric Billoud). They'd been travelling together most of the time, anyway. "It took the pressure off. The race became more social and enjoyable." Cromwell went on to win.

He went to Cairns for the EcoChallenge. "I enjoyed parts of it, I'd never done anything so long. I learned a lot and applied it through the race. But the Southern Traverse is still my favourite — the terrain and the companionship, catching up with people you only see once a year. There's an amazing camaraderie among the teams. It can be a very social race but not this year."

He also learned some valuable lessons in Brazil, where he won that country's first adventure race, the Mata Atlantica, shortly before the Traverse. "I was relying on the compass too much. We had old maps with many roads marked. At one point we had to take a road after 50 metres and descend but I had us climbing. We went back and took the other one. I learned a lot from Tania Pearce who follows more what is happening on the map."

So, come the 1998 Traverse, Hadyn lines up at the start with his old life saving mates, Aiden Craig and Tim Grammer, in Long International, so named because of the amount of time Aiden felt he owed his employers.

"We were determined to enjoy ourselves. We realised we had good skills and a good chance if we minimised mistakes and stoppages. We knew we should do okay but that 'okay' was never 'we should win.' We never thought that until we reached Lake Te Anau, then it was, 'We've done well so far, let's not blow it.'"

The Southern Traverse has changed a lot, he feels, it's got longer with tighter organisation but there's still room for improvement.

"It has got to a length where mental strength is most important. It's not a bunny race, I think it's a good length, a technical race and not a sprint, with a good balance between the physical and mental."

The problem now is that most of the people doing the Southern Traverse have similar physical abilities. "The difference is mental. You need to decide when you're going to sleep and where. We slept a lot in the field, two minutes here, five minutes there, and saved the longer sleeps for the TAs. Looking back, we should have slept more and slept earlier." Again, just like two years earlier.

"Training is continually being adapted with what I've learned. I'm always listening to other peoples' ideas and integrating them with what I've already learned. Physically, a background in disciplined training has been very important. That developed younger for me with swimming, getting up early, biking to the pool to swim before school.

"The first couple of years when I got into multisport I did a lot of stuff that was longer, up to 30 hours a week, not including overnight trips that I don't really see as training but at the end of the day it is. It's training for an event[like the Southern Traverse].

"For '98 I probably spent less time training than ever because I'm getting a lot smarter and because my base is so much stronger. I did the hours and hours in earlier years, now I just have to maintain the base wisely.

"Training smarter means being more specific. For example, rather than go for a two hour run, do a two hour hike uphill with a heavy pack. You don't do a lot of running in races like the Southern Traverse although there are sections where you can do a bit of jogging. You used to be able to run when the race was shorter but now, up around four days, you can't afford to do so much running. The same applies with paddling, you're better off on rivers than paddling up and down [the flat water of] Frankton Arm. Get your skills together in the water and you'll probably enjoy yourself a lot more. Doing the same two hour paddle every second day would probably drive you mad. Rather than do a 4-5 hour slog in one day, try two shorter sessions and then a weekend away in the hills, playing with your skills, reading the land, route finding and using the compass."

Until recently, Hadyn hadn't been so strong in navigation. It's only in the last 18 months he's begun to play with compasses, "something I find fascinating, challenging and enjoyable. I started with the basics, shooting and following bearings and relying on the compass. Now it comes down more to what's happening on the map, reasoning with the map, reading the contours and getting a feel for the land to find where you are. For example, to find Blue Hankie Corner there was constant reassessment of where we were on the map while following a bearing — the lie of the land, which way the rivers flow, there's so much information out there. We tried to take it all in and visualise where we were on the map."

Preparing himself for the event, Hadyn set himself an exercise. He'd choose a random point on a map and then try to visualise the horizons at north, south, east and west. Would the ridge line be broad or sharp? What lies before it? And so on.

In earlier races, he'd been getting lost and not knowing where he was. "It leaves a pretty hollow feeling in your gut." And, of course, if you don't know where you are, how do you find your way out?

"In the '98 Traverse, we made an effort to know where we were all the time and we made joint decisions when we were tired or unsure exactly where we were."

Is there a special nutrition regime?

"I've come back to just eating what I really feel like. But I've begun eating a lot more protein and my diet has become more balanced.

"And coffee, of course, you've got to drink a lot of coffee," he adds with a gust of laughter.

But what happens in a race? Is there a special race diet or menu?

"There's a list of transition food [another of Hadyn's lists] but it's up to the support crew what they'll offer although we may request something for the next Transition Area. It's most important to eat something you're going to enjoy. Eat Power Bars and the like and you soon get sick of them. We race a lot with sandwiches, savoury crackers and beer sticks as well as bars and bits and pieces like that. I ate a lot of scroggin this year."

Hadyn and his team also had a system worked out for the Transition Areas that they stuck to throughout. "We made a point of eating as soon as we arrived, as we sat down and before we got old clothes off and a fresh set on, before we looked at the map [for the next section]." It may have been Complan or a tin of creamed rice, it was just something to go straight into the stomach and allowed the support crew to prepare other food while the racers got ready for the next leg.

"The crew worked out a *bain marie* system that would keep food hot for hours, if necessary. And then we had warm water to wash in, too. Last year we had burned sausages and overcooked food. This year the food was fantastic."

Is this another 'secret weapon' in Hadyn's arsenal?

"Hydration is terribly important. If you feel you need a drink, you're probably too late. One of us was wanting a pee every 10 or 15 minutes."

But that, unfortunately, leads to another problem. The constant sipping from a Camelback tends to strip enamel off the teeth and put blisters on the tongue. "I hadn't thought much about oral hygiene before but have now found gargling salt water at TAs to be a very good idea."

On the feet, Hadyn uses Vaseline liberally on the toes and heels and wears gaiters in the tramping sections to keep out dirt, sticks and stones.

"Early in the race, I try to treat blisters as soon as I feel them coming on. In the last few hours I don't worry so much. Personally, I like to pop my blisters, get the liquid out. For me, it relieves pressure and perhaps stops their spread. Apparently, if you leave a piece of cotton in the blister it will continually drain."

But, because of the increased risk of infection, he's not sure he'd recommend this — or try it himself.

In the EcoChallenge in Cairns, Hadyn was able to put his blister remedies to real test. "In the first hour and a half, we stopped to fix Tane Humphrey's feet. But towards the end of the race, when other teams had huge problems, we had none. We had nipped the problem in the bud.

"This year in the Traverse I didn't have feet problems except the last two or three hours alongside Lake Mavora. But we ran that, we just wanted to get to the Transition Area."

Besides the sore and swollen feet on the last mountain bike ride, Hadyn also had nasty chafing and "so wore two pairs of cycling shorts. I shouldn't have had any chafing. It came from wearing cycle shorts on the previous walk. Looser, baggy shorts, even no undies to let the air circulate, is the best system." To ease chafing, Hadyn finds that for him natural lubricants work better than petroleum based products.

On the question of drugs, he is adamant. "You're on such a natural high anyway, I just don't know why anyone would want to use drugs. Every moment is enjoyable. Maybe in the shorter races but I think it's a relatively clean sport."

And how, exactly, does Hadyn see the future of adventure racing?

"It is becoming more professional, certainly more commercial. With sponsorship you may be able to make a career out of it. I haven't ever made money out of a race but I think it's getting to the stage where it's possible. Perhaps you can cover expenses in the smaller events and make a few dollars in the likes of the Raid or the Eco.

"I haven't heard good things about the last Eco. People liked the country but not the race. It's becoming too set up for TV and not the racers. That's why the Southern Traverse is still my favourite, it remains a competitors' race."

Bill Godsall — an original

Bill Godsall is one of the 'originals.' His grit, determination, adaptability, humour, warmth and friendliness epitomise the spirit of both the Southern Traverse and adventure racing in general. Having competed in every Southern Traverse, for three wins, one in a five-person outfit and two in three-man teams, he is one of the most successful competitors.

But not in 1998. Bill's Team Cromwell was one of those shivering the night away waiting for the streams to go down on the second mountain bike section, putting them well behind the front three, and then spent hours looking for the phantom Check Point on the Takitimus trek. "We had mental problems. We thought,'Where's the CP?' There was a constant undermining and we didn't fire like in the past. It got better towards the end and we had very good Transition Area times — and a great support crew."

It's all relative, of course. The team went through every TA in fourth, fifth or sixth place and eventually finished fifth over all.

Bill had had no plans to compete in that first Traverse. He was a marathon runner, with a best time of 2:25, and regularly running 160km a week. His fitness was never in question and some of the local boys needed another person for their team. So Bill bought a kayak and two bikes, one for the road and one for the trails, and started training in the new disciplines.

He recalls that first race: "There was a gnarly storm on the lake and we lost one member to hypothermia. We'd started competitively but with the delay over the hypothermia we fell back to 16th and, of course, were unranked.

"Those early races were hard, with great rafting sections, twice on the Shotover and the Landsborough. The hardness is still there but the athletes have changed, especially this year. Skill levels are up and more people are on a similar level although some teams are still grossly underskilled. The more experienced teams have immense talents, they've been learning navigation skills and doing more racing to polish their skills. This year, we were stuck at night at that river for only three hours but in that time, heaps of teams caught up. Okay, we got away from them reasonably comfortably, but in previous years they wouldn't have caught us."

Cycling and kayaking clubs, he feels, have been benefiting from the boom in multisports with many athletes signing up to improve their abilities. So, as overall skill levels improve, "what makes a difference is the ability to tolerate, to cope with a lack of sleep. Just look at the times out on the course, they weren't so different. But teams were sleeping four, six or even eight hours in the transitions. You just don't need that amount of sleep. People don't have enough faith in themselves."

Bill also sees a definite relationship between fitness and the amount of sleep needed. Teams that want to win will only sleep three or four hours in total while others dream on for six to eight hours every night.

"It's a bloody fine line, eh? You don't really need that sleep. The fitter you are the less sleep you need to keep going. This year only one member of our team needed to sleep. I think we only had about three hours sleep in total and I didn't feel at any stage I really needed more than that. If you're fit, you can keep going with a little bit less sleep. It does affect your decision making but you get used to it. The years I spent doing shift work helped me."

Even so, Bill doesn't get it right all the time. He's done the EcoChallenge three times. "I enjoyed British Columbia. It was a tough race. We made a bad navigation mistake on the first day and had to fight our way back through the field. Only four teams finished the full course. We were fourth. It's interesting, too, that of those first 20 athletes, nine were Kiwis.

"In Cairns, we were running first or second but a lack of sleep cost us at the end." His team was fifth. And in Morocco, they were unranked finally because one team member fell victim to altitude sickness.

Despite his overseas experience, Bill still finds the Traverse a great race, "a bare bones adventure race where you have to rely on yourself. It's not quite international [like the Raid and EcoChallenge] but it's good to see teams from other countries coming here." But, he wonders, "Is the terrain here too tough [for the internationals]?"

Although the course is different every year, there are basic similarities, he finds. But "it was good to get away from road biking. You used to win or lose on the run. The trekking section is still important but because it's longer there's less actual running and navigation has become more important. You also need good skills on the mountain bike and kayak. You might not get the winning break but you can get left behind." Having said all that, he admits the bike legs played a big part this year.

He does have one problem, however. "Nowadays, we're all trapped into having to move the same way, the same route. This year the only real choice was between Te Anau and Mavora Lakes and most of us went low and long, the easier route."

What about the missing Check Point in the Takitimus? "That was a mental thing, we couldn't get our heads around it. We didn't know if we were disqualified, we were still in the race or if there would be a time penalty for missing the CP."

Looking back, two Traverses have special places in Bill's memory. "That first race was such a big adventure. You can't imagine what it's like until you do it. Some people will get a hell of a fright." And the second race he also remembers fondly because "it was a very special five man team."Coming home first must have helped, too.

He also recalls the '94 Traverse when his three-man team (with Jim Cotter and Ian Edmonds) was bonded by the elements. "We were very frightened on Wakatipu. There were huge waterspouts reaching up from the lake surface and enormous waves. We were paddling right into a headwind, trying to ferry glide across the lake. Ian was paddling flat out and going backwards. 'What am I going to do?' asked Ian. 'You're doing everything,' said Jim. 'Just keep going.' We were too scared to turn into the transition because that would have meant turning across the waves."

The support crew could see it all. They were terrified and helpless as they watched "our boys" disappearing and reappearing through the waves.

Eventually the team screwed up the courage to do it, made the final passage to the transition safely and went on to win.

While Kiwi adventure racers remain the best in Bill's estimation, "the rest of the world is catching up fast. The Spanish are gutsy athletes and the Finns had very good paddling in the Eco. They're good cyclists, too. If they polish up their trekking they'll be very good. Some of the Kiwis are starting to get egos, they think they're going to win by right, but no way."

He is not so complimentary about the Americans, however, except the women. "They're good, stronger than Kiwi women, but the men do a lot of their training in the gym. They look good, they're powerful, awesome looking athletes, especially compared to the leaner Kiwis, but when you get out there, they're a bit soft when it matters."

To compete successfully in adventure racing, Bill says, you need a high level of basic fitness, "an endurance base is the most important thing."

He has this in spades from his years as a marathon runner. "Ten years of running 160km a week has given me a huge endurance base and it's easier for me to get back up to a reasonable performance peak. I train reasonably hard for the EcoChallenge, for the Southern Traverse and for the Coast to Coast. Add that up over a year and the level is pretty high. I may need to sharpen skills but that's about all."

"I still do most of my training by running," he says. "It's a great way to build up the heart and lungs, much faster than, say, cycling. An hour of running is about the same as two and a half hours cycling."

Just the same, he has to fit all his training round work and family. "I run and ride the bike for up to two or three hours. I also go out for the odd weekend thrash but it has to fit in with the family lifestyle. I'm not totally convinced of the need for overnight treks although it works for some people. These group treks might be what has made many teams so much stronger. We've never been able to do that. The team only gets together at race time [team member Jim Cotter now lives in Australia]. We have to rely on each other to train hard."

Bill is one who doesn't feel the need for high levels of specific training but, when pushed, does agree that skill levels are very important. Especially navigation.

"Navigation is becoming more important and perhaps that's why some of these teams have closed the gap. They have orienteers on them now. If you got lost and spent three hours catching up, that would have cost you three or four places this year. Other years it might not have been so critical, we might have been able to run the trekking sections. Now we just walk fast. We're good mountain runners and we used to be able to run away from most other teams but not now. It is becoming more and more critical to choose the right route.

"And you need kayak skills because in these races now, if you don't have them you can drown. There's no two ways about it."

Where diet is concerned, Bill does say it is important to keep the weight down. "What's the point of buying the latest lightweight kayak or bike if you're already carrying extra weight?"

"I'd be lying if I said I had a special diet. I used to [laughter]. I eat every kind of junk food going, including the odd packet of biscuits and fish and chips maybe once a week, but I have 20 years of training behind me and I've had a gutsful of fad diets. As long as you've got a fair idea of what calories you're putting in and what calories you're burning then you won't put on too much weight. I think you can go overboard on diet. After 20 years, it's just an all-round, healthy diet. The same old story, lots of fruit and vegetables."

When racing, his rucksack is filled with fruit cake, baked potatoes, scroggin, sandwiches and fruitbars plus the usual Power Bars and Leppin for energy boosts.

"The thing about Power Bars, sports bars or Leppin, you can carry a lot of them in a small area and so they're not a lot of weight and they're the maximum horsepower you can get for what you put in. You do need a lot of fluid but all these races are held where there are lots of streams so it doesn't matter that much."

He acknowledges, however, that many people have turned off Power Bars and the like "because they hate the taste. I don't know why the manufacturers don't get on to that. Jim just hates them, he won't eat them. He had a lot of fruit bars."

And when he reaches each Transition Area, he has "a cup of coffee, always a cup of coffee."

Feet, not surprisingly with his background as a runner, are an area of particular concern to Bill and until the EcoChallenge in British Columbia, he'd never had problems. There, his feet were a mess. Now he uses barrier cream to stop blisters but, he says, "you need to find out before the race what will happen to your feet and remedy it. Make sure you've tried it in practice."

"Footwear is extremely important. There's a lot available now and it's not just one brand that's really, really good. You just need something that's wide, to allow for swelling and spreading so you don't get hot spots, and maybe a little longer than normal. It's taken me eight Traverses to learn that [laughter].

"I don't have a special adventure racing shoe, just a running shoe because it's comfortable and drains well. That's important. Water's the thing that kills your feet, they go soft and wrinkly. The barrier cream is a big help."

Looking to the future, he sees adventure racing becoming more professional with good money for the winners. If you've got a good team, guys like [Steve] Gurney, [Keith] Murray and [John] Howard, you can make money because prize money's bloody good. But if you don't win the race, you're lucky to recoup your entry fee.

Presently, however, Bill sees a money barrier and he would like to see the cost come down for competitors. "Spud [Bill's wife Irene, as almost nobody knows her] says I'm being conservative but I reckon I've spent about $20,000 on gear in the last three years. That's a lot of money that hasn't been available to the family, for the kids' activities."

The EcoChallenge will in future require national teams and he feels there should be a selection process to decide on the three New Zealand teams permitted. Then there should be a reserve list in case selected athletes can't go. Besides, he says, "if New Zealanders don't start pulling together they're going to lose their advantage, lose their number one status."

And how does Bill see the Southern Traverse compared with, say, the EcoChallenge? "I think it's a great race, it's still just the bare bones, an adventure race. You can't rely on the back up because it's just not going to be there. You have to have the skills yourself. Like, in the Eco, if you fall down, somebody will come along and put a sticking plaster on you but in the Southern Traverse, if you fall down, you get yourself up.

"And that's what adventure racing basically is.

"The Southern Traverse isn't a true international race yet, we're not getting the top international teams here although they keep talking about it. It would be good to see some of the top teams coming out here, to see how they do. Maybe the terrain's too tough for them. They might get into the top five but I don't think they'd make it into the top three."

Bill has one particular adventure racing story he recounts often. Like all the best stories it plumbs the depths but has a happy ending and provides a salutary lesson.

"My worst moment in adventure racing would have to be during the EcoChallenge in British Columbia. Kristina [Strode-Penny], Ian [Edmonds], Jim [Cotter], Eric [Billoud] and I were pushing really hard, trying to make up lost time [after a navigation error]. We'd completed a hard paddle with very little sleep, just a cat nap and then not everybody slept. We kept pushing very hard on the road and gravel mountain bike course. It was only about 76 kms and undulating and we thought it would be fast and simple. Then there was a lost map, which Eric had to go back 20 minutes for, and a disagreement over whose fault the loss was. There were continual stops which frustrated those who were in good shape (I wasn't!) and constant falling onto the tar seal — Jim suffered worst here — and finally a broken chain after a crash that took longer to fix than it should have. We were all hallucinating and we had trouble finding our actual location on the map. Finding the Check Point was easy, after that.

"Because we'd all struggled so much, due entirely to lack of sleep, we decided to get some much needed rest. Ian woke us again to get going and he and Eric marched off up the road with their bikes, I struggled to pack up my gear and Jim followed the other two without his bike, still very much asleep. I ran after them to stop progress while Jim was woken. We all went back to help Jim pack and get his bike and then we found Kris still sitting at the CP. She was very disappointed with what had gone on the previous night.

"As a team and, more importantly, as a group of very close friends, we sat down and talked about each other's strengths and their key contributions to the team. We then struggled through the last 16km to the Transition Area and a welcome meal prepared by our support crew.

"This story always sticks in my mind. Here was a close knit group of friends, who, personally, I was in awe of, and we'd all come unstuck big time, mentally and physically. It killed any ego lingering in us and said, in the clearest possible terms: 'Welcome to big time adventure racing.'

"There's been a special bond connecting all of us since that race ended."

And, finally, why does he keep doing it, why does he go out in the wind, the rain, the snow and the sun, over mountains and down rivers? "I love to push myself. I enjoy being competitive and I've met so many great people and made so many lifetime friends, how can I not keep doing it? Besides, there's another win coming up. I feel it!"

First Family

The second generation of adventure racers has been competing for three years. Adventure racing may be only 10 years old but multisport is older. Most competitors in both branches of the sport grew up playing traditional sports. Many branched into triathlon and so into multisport or others came from tramping and hunting backgrounds and went straight into adventure racing.

But there is a new generation competing now, a second generation that has grown up with multisport as a normal activity. There is no better example of this than the Prince family of Christchurch.

Russell was in the winning team in that first Grand Traverse but then pulled back, concentrating more on his running. He competed with great success in every Coast to Coast from 1985 to 1998 and also the first two Southern Traverses. He's raced up Mt Kinabalu, the highest peak in South East Asia, and in the Mt Everest Marathon. Ultra-running became a passion and he broke the Oceania 100km record.

Viv Prince — lifestyle

His wife Viv was part of his support crew on that first Coast to Coast, assisted by a two-year-old. But Viv thought competing looked more fun than assisting and so next year she came back in a team — and took out first place. She had entered the realms of multisport.

At school, Viv had participated in a number of sports, hockey, netball, tennis, gymnastics, lifesaving and softball, but her principal interest was judo, begun when a girlfriend asked her along for company. In the next eight years she went on to win national junior titles and compete in the Oceania championships. "I think it was the discipline of judo that gave me the mental and physical toughness required for adventure racing."

The judo stopped for two reasons. She got married and began a family and she was also aware of the long term injuries affecting the older judokas. For the next 10 years she applied herself to her three children — and all that implies — did a number of polytech and craft courses and built a house. Holidays and spare weekends were spent in the mountains, climbing and tramping from her family's holiday home at Arthur's Pass.

Then, in 1984, Viv and Russell stumbled upon a group of bedraggled individuals at Klondyke Corner, just down the road from Arthur's Pass village. They were, of course, competitors in the second Coast to Coast.

After her supporting role in 1985, she went for a mountain run with a girlfriend considering individual competition in the Coast to Coast after entering as a team the year before. She had no answer to Viv's skills in the rough, hopping from boulder to boulder. Viv excelled, she was in her element, and so a team was formed.

Needing to improve her fitness, she began running round the park until her team mate reminded her: "We're out to win, you know." It was time for Viv to extricate the proverbial digit. She began running tramping tracks and up the Port Hills and bought an old bike. That was a revelation, the discovery she could actually ride up the hills without the lycra. She still remembers that first race clearly, especially waiting at the traffic lights for a rival woman with whom she'd made a pact when they both realised they couldn't shake the other off. Viv did manage that at the finish, of course.

She also remembers clearly bunches of guys drafting off the pair of women.

All in all, she now has nine Coast to Coasts under her belt, including four one-dayers since 1993. She's won three team titles, one with elder daughter Jackie, and the two day individual in 1989.

Like Russell, she has competed in the Mt Kinabalu Climbathon. In four starts she's taken third, fourth and sixth and also been first international woman home. In the Mt Everest Marathon she broke the previous world record — but still had to settle for second place.

When the first Southern Traverse started from Lake Ohau in 1991, Viv was there at the start. When she finished, her team was in fourth place. Then she took time out from the Traverse.

At the Raid Gauloises in Sarawak, she whipped an eclectic bunch of neophytes into shape, overcame the problems of stolen gear, and, in the first few days, gave Steve Gurney and John Howard a run for their money. It was her first big adventure race, too. "It was the best thing I could have done. My marriage had not long broken up and the race, before and after, put me in a whole new world and taught me that I could do anything."

She has been a regular competitor in the EcoChallenge. At the first Eco in Utah, she managed third. The next was in British Columbia and there, where only four teams finished the entire course, she was in the winning combination. At Cairns she was third again and in Morocco her team finished fifth place and were lucky to do that after two of their Arab stallions had a vicious and spectacular fight - with the riders still on their backs.

But in 1996 she was back in the Southern Traverse in an international team. A couple of weeks before the event, the team's navigator, an Alaskan, had to pull out after suffering frost bite while training. There's a minimum age requirement of 18 in the Traverse but an untried 16-year-old was given special dispensation to compete — because he had his mother in the same team to keep an eye on him. If she could keep up.

In 1997, Viv was part of the Team Macpac line-up that battled through the cyclonic winds sent along that year by *el Niño* . It was Viv and her team mates who battled the snow this book began with. On the other side of that pass they made a serious error of judgement, bypassing the Check Point on the top abseil (and had to spend several hours going back to it), that cost them the win overall but they were still the first 5-person team home.

The last Traverse was a disaster from Team Macpac's point of view. They'd been moving well, keeping up with the leaders and keeping every one honest, when one team member came down with a chest infection, forcing the team's withdrawal. Viv and her team mates stayed on, however, with 'mum' keeping a proud eye, from a respectful distance, on her 'little boy' Aaron, back for the second time in another international team.

So what has driven Viv to be one of the world's top adventure racers? Sitting at home and waiting for things to happen is not in her make-up. She likes to take life firmly in her own hands and give it a good shake to see what falls out. Adventure racing appeals because of the challenge and excitement. The Southern Traverse takes her through her beloved New Zealand back country but international races offer the addition of exotic cultures, new people and stunning landscapes.

It is, in a word, a lifestyle, a lifestyle that gives her the passion and excitement she has come to love. She likes to be fit and competitive, so adventure racing allows her to train where she wants to be, in the outdoors, and then test herself in sometimes exotic locations among people who share her feelings.

An adventure racer, says Viv, "needs to be curious, willing to give things a go and seek new challenges. She — or he — has to be physically fit with great endurance and mentally very strong which is why tramping or hunting is a better background than triathlon. Both activities involve extended periods in the wilderness, developing natural instincts, navigation and the ability to cope with adverse conditions and heavy loads. It is also necessary to enjoy working in a team." It is little wonder, then, that Viv has such a formidable record.

To keep fit, Viv cycles (currently she doesn't own a car so this is also a necessity), runs and paddles her kayak on a regular basis. She likes to get out on weekends for long, demanding trips or on occasion, will do one big day, "a mega training trip" and that family holiday home in Arthur's Pass makes a perfect base. But while that is the ideal, all training sessions, and the races themselves, have to be fitted around the demands of family, friends and work.

Each race, she finds, she learns something new, about herself or ways to do things better, and this has to be incorporated into her training. Weaker skills have to be worked on and improved and a new race may throw up a discipline she has no experience in. In the time available, she then has to learn how to do it and become proficient. Horse riding is a good example.

Viv likes to maintain a healthy, mixed diet including whole grains, lots of fruit and vegetables and protein. She will use some vitamin supplements during training and definitely while racing. She also feels there may be a link between her vitamin intake and the lack of mouth ulcers, that adventure racers' curse. To ensure there's no anaemia, a common problem among female athletes, she has iron injections and periodic checks.

During a race, she has carbohydrate supplements available but much prefers and craves real food. Support crew in the Southern Traverse and Raid Gauloises can provide good, nutritious meals with plenty of fresh ingredients. In events like the EcoChallenge, where there are now no assistants and everything has to be pre-packaged, noodles and dehydrated foods come into their own. When time is crucial (and isn't that any time during a race?), water is added to the food and the package put in place next to the body to allow body heat to help the food preparation. It's fast but can be messy if packets aren't sealed properly. Dried fruit and nuts taste good but she finds them heavy to carry. Power bars she likes especially when she's kayaking. She also gets a craving for savoury things as the sodium gets flushed from her body so to satisfy that need for salt she carries salty snacks. Canned fruits and stews have their place and chocolate is eaten "now and again." Lollies, too, are "something to chew on."

Whether training or racing, Viv has a policy of tending to niggles immediately they're felt and the same with injuries. If it is a sprain, she will strap it and back off the pace. Stretching and massage are important and she has found chiropractic so beneficial that with her youngest child now 17-years-old she has embarked on a full time, five year course of study to become a chiropractor herself. Now there's belief in a system!

Like most adventure racers, Viv pays special attention to her feet. Swelling will soon make regular size shoes too small, leading to chafing and blisters. She has also been experimenting a lot with socks, finding that some materials are better for her than others but does say that you should always experiment with new socks (or shoes or any equipment for that matter) well before the race. Blisters are more likely to occur in two situations, she finds. The first is in the heat but curiously, she had no problems in Morocco and puts that down to a new generation of light, sturdy shoes made specifically for adventure racing. She felt they gave more protection. And they would undoubtedly help in the second situation, too, where heavier packs lead to faster deterioration in the feet.

But what is it like, being a woman with three or four men?

It's important to be in a team with similar goals and ideals, she finds, preferably friends. But "the imbalance of gender can sometimes make it difficult. Individual personalities have a lot of bearing but often men and women think and communicate differently. Sometimes women approach problems from a different angle or perspective." She remembers a team training trip when she struggled up a hill, wondering why nobody helped her when she would help anybody else suffering. At a team talk later, one of the guys commented: "If anyone's struggling, you have to tell us otherwise we won't know."

Viv is also adamant that "just because you're a woman, don't think you're necessarily going to be the slowest or the weakest. Everyone goes through bad patches, through tiredness, lack of food or water, pushing too hard or injury and sickness. Often, towards the end of a race, the woman is the strongest, has the better endurance.

"Break the race into sections, aim for the next check point or the race will consume you. Remember a change of discipline or the coming dawn will give you a new lease of life. Stay positive, relish your surroundings and feel privileged to be where you are."

Despite the mid-life change in career and the demands that will make on her time, Viv is not yet ready to give up adventure racing. The Southern Traverse is always attractive but in particular now she is eyeing Sweden in the year 2000.

As for adventure racing itself, she sees continued growth. "There will be more and more big races and they will probably become more commercial. The number of teams on the waiting lists shows that already there are not enough races for the number of racers wanting to do them." On the question of professional adventure racers, she is a bit cagey, saying "it's more of a life-style. It would be a shame if the prize money got too big."

When, finally, Viv does hang up her racing shoes, there's no way she'll be able to keep out of involvement in the sport.

Aaron is already leading the way in the second generation of adventure racers. And Lara is a keen runner, a good cyclist and loves adventure. She already shows great endurance but is starting slowly. So far she has limited herself to 24 hour rogaines and the Coast to Coast but she is starting to eye shorter adventure races very keenly, especially in a women's team with her mother.

Perhaps in the not too distant future they'll need a new category of family teams in adventure racing.

Aaron Prince — second generation

"Ever since I can remember," says 19-year-old Aaron Prince, "my sisters and I used to go and 'help' at the races mum [Viv Prince] and dad competed in." This was not what you would call a typical Kiwi upbringing where ball sports and boats seem to be prominent.

"From about the age of 10, I started competing in some of the shorter races, often in teams. I began to be about as quick as mum when I could fit into her shoes and now that my feet are bigger than dad's, I occasionally beat him, too."

The very best adventure racers today are in the 35 to 45-years-old bracket. They have come to the sport from a background in other pursuits or love of the outdoors. Aaron is in the vanguard of the second generation of adventure racers, those who have grown up with the sport. While still in his teens he is keeping his mentors honest, pushing them hard in the shorter events and not too far behind the leaders in the multi-day races. The Southern Traverse at four and a half days is his longest race to date. Sensibly, he has goals other than the EcoChallenge and the Raid at the moment, recognising he needs the stamina (he already shows the mental strength) that comes with age and experience.

"I'll take it as it comes," he says, "and I don't expect that I'll always — or only — do adventure races. They're too hard! I don't think it would be a good idea for me to do any of the major international adventure races for a few years yet. The first time I did the [Southern] Traverse in '96, I didn't feel quite right for about three or four months after when I was competing in other races. After the Traverse last year I got sick the next week and took at least a few weeks after that to come right. I've now done the Coast to Coast and been quite run down since that.

"About two weeks after one of these races I feel like I've recovered again but when I try to do some of the things I normally do, I find I'm still not fully recovered. Maybe when I'm a bit older I'll have more stamina and doing these multi-day races won't knock me around so much.

"Learning to be an adventure racer seems to be an ever ongoing thing and the people who seem to know what they're doing have been involved in outdoor activities for most of their lives. Most of the top adventure racers seem to be about 35 to 40 plus years old."

All of which goes to show one of the major reasons why young Aaron shows such precocious ability. It is not just his physical prowess. He is intelligent and uses his brain, he thinks carefully about what is going on around him. It is fascinating to reflect on what he might be capable of, even by his mid- to late-20s, still years before the current crop of racers are at their peak.

At the moment — and to his credit — adventure races are really only a secondary interest. His first love is orienteering, which he began a little over three years ago when "mum took me along to local orienteering races. My first major result was during my last year at high school in the secondary school nationals in 1997 when, much to my and everyone else's surprise, I narrowly came home first. In 1997 I also won the Canterbury

Championships and came second in 1998 [racing against adventure racing supremos like Steve Gurney, John Howard and Keith Murray].

"This year I'm planning on going to the Junior World Orienteering Championships in Bulgaria in July. Last year a couple of Kiwis came in the top 20 at the JWOC and I would be very pleased to do as well as they did. I don't think I will, though, because they are a lot quicker than me and it was their third time over there."

He's also done several 6, 12 and 24 hour rogaines, beginning with a 6 hour at the age of 12 with his older sister Jackie. Last year he completed a 12 hour rogaine with Keith Murray. "I couldn't understand how he managed to get up all the hills so fast and also get tangled up in nearly every fence we crossed." But that's why Murray is one of the very best adventure racers, whatever happens he still sets the pace. Aaron has also done 24 hour events with his mother's EcoChallenge team, John Howard, his "little sister Lara" and others.

It is all vital training for adventure racing where navigation — orienteering — has become the pre-eminent skill.

While at school, his sporting interests generally related to multisport. In secondary school competition, he was the Canterbury cross-country champion in 1996, triathlon champion in 1996 and 1997, second in the duathlon in 1997 and won the steeplechase that year. He was also the winner at the New Zealand Secondary Schools Multisports Championships in 1996.

Somewhat surprisingly, he has shown little interest in the Coast to Coast, the seminal multi-day multisport race in New Zealand. In 1998 he entered in a team for 12th place. This year he tried it as an individual, coming home a very creditable second in the 2-day event.

Despite his obvious talents and the example of his mother, his two Southern Traverse entries were unplanned, last minute affairs.

In 1996 he was given a special dispensation because of his age (just 16-years-old) and allowed to join his mother's 5-person international team. In the end, Aaron, who'd only recently started orienteering seriously, assumed the mantle of team navigator, sharing duties with mum Viv. Because he always maintains a high state of fitness and was skilled in the required disciplines, he helped to bring the team home fourth in the 5-person category. And paid for it physically for a long time afterwards.

It was the same again last year. Two weeks before the race American Isaac Wilson confirmed a sponsor — he just needed to make up a team. Fit, ready and with the time to spare, Aaron joined the team, a 3-man unit on this occasion. They never looked like winning, they never caused the front teams much concern, but they put in a steady performance to come in ninth overall.

Most individuals — and teams — spend months preparing for an adventure race. They have carefully crafted training programmes leading to a peak for the race. So how does a teenager, seemingly far too young to be an adventure racer, show a clean pair of heels to the majority of the contestants and without any special training for the race? You wonder what he might do if he trained specifically for an event.

Clearly he cannot be your average racer. His upbringing , for a start, precludes that and his multisport results while still at school are a further indication of his ability. He runs, often with a compass as in orienteering events and rogaines, paddles and cycles on a regular basis, building up that fitness and endurance base that is critical to successful adventure racing. "Normally, I just do what I feel like doing. I am a great fan of resting if I don't feel right. I don't like having a set programme of what I have to do. If I have a race coming up, I usually decide in my head how much I want to train for that particular race and change things as I go. On most weekends there is usually some race or some sort of activity to keep me busy." And in peak condition.

"I think the way I learn the most useful skills for adventure racing is by doing orienteering races. The best way to learn a lot is to spend time with experienced people or even race with them. I could probably learn a fair bit from mum but unfortunately, because she is my mother, I don't tend to listen to her that well!" Ah, how true, I hear parents lamenting.

During racing and training he has learned to deal with niggles and minor problems promptly, before they flare up into major disasters. If he sustains an injury, he doesn't like to mask the hurt with painkillers. "Usually, if you are hurting you should take notice, not try to stop the pain by taking drugs. I don't like to take drugs such as painkillers unless it is absolutely necessary."

Nor is he in favour of caffeine, guarana and the like during a long race, fearing the payback. "If you get on a high from those things now," he says, "you'll be on a low later." And it goes without saying the low zone can be more harmful than any temporary benefits gained.

What then, does he think of adventure racing and the people who take part in it?

"I've only done the Traverse so I'm no expert. I like the way everyone seems pretty casual and friendly and that makes it different from a lot of the other non-adventure races I've done. It is the type of people who compete that makes the race.

"Adventure racers are all easygoing and nothing bothers them. They all seem to have achieved a lot in their lives aside from adventure racing. Most of all, they are extremely modest." Just as Aaron is.

Appendix

If you're looking for kayak or mountain bike clubs in your area, you could try:

New Zealand Canoeing Federation
PO Box 63
Waikanae
04-293 1585

New Zealand Mountain Bike Association
PO Box 361
Timaru
03-684 5965

Useful sites on the World Wide Web include:
www.southerntraverse.com
www.raidgauloises.com
www.ecochallenge.com
www.elf-adventure.com
www.beyondadventure.com
(This last site has some very interesting links.)

Figure 1

PERIODISATION

COMPONENTS & TRAINING